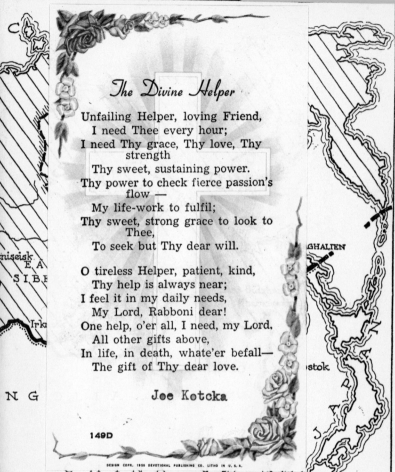

The Divine Helper

Unfailing Helper, loving Friend,
  I need Thee every hour;
I need Thy grace, Thy love, Thy
    strength
  Thy sweet, sustaining power.
Thy power to check fierce passion's
    flow —
  My life-work to fulfil;
Thy sweet, strong grace to look to
    Thee,
  To seek but Thy dear will.

O tireless Helper, patient, kind,
  Thy help is always near;
I feel it in my daily needs,
  My Lord, Rabboni dear!
One help, o'er all, I need, my Lord,
  All other gifts above,
In life, in death, whate'er befall—
  The gift of Thy dear love.

Joe Kotcka

149D

DESIGN COPR. 1956 DEVOTIONAL PUBLISHING CO. LITHO IN U.S.A.

The Uzbek Soviet Socialist Republic
The Tadjik Soviet Socialist Republic
The Kazakh Soviet Socialist Republic
The Kirghiz Soviet Socialist Republic

The five Republics added in 1940 are not included in this map.
The Latvian Soviet Socialist Republic
The Lithuanian Soviet Socialist Republic
The Estonian Soviet Socialist Republic
The Karelian-Finnish Soviet Socialist Republic
The Moldavian Soviet Socialist Republic

It would be difficult to think of a happier or more timely combination of author and subject than the Webbs on Soviet Russia. Eight years ago, after close to a half-century of writing on society and social reform, they first published their searching analysis *Soviet Communism, A New Civilization?* — a study generally regarded as the first serious attempt of major proportions to break through the emotional thinking about Russia to the fundamental aims and accomplishment of this so large-scale social experiment.

This volume is a distillation of the earlier work. It contains an evaluation of the Soviet Constitution of 1936 and a description of Soviet Communism in operation in terms of social, political, economic and religious purposes and practices. There follows the complete text of the Constitution translated by Anna Louise Strong, and finally a short summary of the Constitution "in terms enabling the British or American reader more easily to comprehend its purport." There is also a crisp sketch of the Webbs by their life-long friend George Bernard Shaw.

The fact that we are today fighting side by side with Soviet Russia against the Axis Powers brings to a head a question which we can no longer put off answering: What are the social aims of the U.S.S.R. and do these aims and the political means for achieving them contain a basis for cooperation between the U.S.S.R. and the United States? This straightforward and lucid discussion will help us come to grips with this question.

THE TRUTH

ABOUT

SOVIET RUSSIA

BY

SIDNEY AND BEATRICE WEBB

WITH AN ESSAY ON THE WEBBS BY
BERNARD SHAW

and a Summary of the Constitution and Working
of Soviet Communism: A New Civilisation *by*
BEATRICE WEBB

LONGMANS, GREEN AND CO.
NEW YORK · LONDON · TORONTO
1942

LONGMANS, GREEN AND CO.
55 FIFTH AVENUE, NEW YORK

LONGMANS, GREEN AND CO. LTD.
OF PATERNOSTER ROW
43 ALBERT DRIVE, LONDON, S.W. 19
17 CHITTARANJAN AVENUE, CALCUTTA
NICOL ROAD, BOMBAY
36A MOUNT ROAD, MADRAS

LONGMANS, GREEN AND CO.
215 VICTORIA STREET, TORONTO

THE TRUTH ABOUT SOVIET RUSSIA

FIRST EDITION

PUBLISHERS' NOTE

This book is a summary of the conclusions reached by Sidney and Beatrice Webb as to the internal organization of the Soviet Union (1941–1942). It is reprinted, with modifications and additions from the Introduction to the reissue (1941) of their book *Soviet Communism: A New Civilisation*

The article on the Webbs by Bernard Shaw is reprinted from *Picture Post* by permission of the author.

PRINTED IN THE UNITED STATES OF AMERICA

CONTENTS

THE WEBBS

By G. BERNARD SHAW

The Webbs, Sidney and Beatrice, officially The Right Honourable the Baron and Lady Passfield, are a superextraordinary pair. I have never met anyone like them, either separately or in their most fortunate conjunction. Each of them is an English force; and their marriage was an irresistible reinforcement. Only England could have produced them. It is true that France produced the Curies, a pair equally happily matched; but in physics they found an established science and left it so, enriched as it was by their labors; but the Webbs found British Constitutional politics something which nobody had yet dreamt of calling a science or thinking of as such.

When they began, they were face to face with Capitalism and Marxism. Marxism, though it claims to be scientific, and has proved itself a mighty force in the modern world, was then a philosophy propounded by a foreigner without administrative experience, who gathered his facts in the Reading Room of the British Museum, and generalized the human race under the two heads of *bourgeoisie* and proletariat apparently without having ever come into business contact with a living human being.

5

The Quarrel with Capitalism

Capitalism was and is a paper Utopia, the most unreal product of wishful thinking of all the Utopias. By pure logic, without a moment's reference to the facts, it demonstrated that you had only to enforce private contracts and let everybody buy in the cheapest market and sell in the dearest to produce automatically a condition in which there would be no unemployment, and every honest and industrious person would enjoy a sufficient wage to maintain himself and his wife and reproduce his kind, whilst an enriched superior class would have leisure and means to preserve and develop the nation's culture and civilization, and, by receiving more of the national income than they could possibly consume, save all the capital needed to make prosperity increase by leaps and bounds.

What Karl Marx Did

Karl Marx's philosophy had no effect on public opinion here or elsewhere; but when he published the facts as to the condition to which Capitalism had reduced the masses, it was like lifting the lid off hell. Capitalism has not yet recovered from the shock of that revelation, and never will.

Sixty years ago, the Marxian shock was only beginning to operate in England. I had to read *Das Kapital* in a French translation, there being no English version as yet. A new champion of the people, Henry Mayers Hyndman, had met and talked with Karl Marx. They quarrelled, as their habit was, but not before Hyndman had been completely converted by Marx; so his Democratic Federation presently became a Social-Democratic Federation. Socialism, in abeyance since the slaughter of the Paris Commune in 1871, suddenly revived; but Marx, its leader and prophet, died at that moment and left the movement to what leadership it could get.

Socialism was not a new thing peculiar to Marx. John Stuart Mill, himself a convert, had converted others, among them one very remarkable young man and an already famous elderly one. The elderly one was the great poet and craftsman William Morris, who, on reading Mill's early somewhat halfhearted condemnation of communism, at once declared that Mill's verdict was against the evidence, and that people who lived on unearned incomes were plainly "damned thieves." He joined Hyndman, and when the inevitable quarrel ensued, founded The Socialist League.

Sidney Webb, the Prodigy

The younger disciple had followed Mill's conversion and shared it. His name was Sidney Webb. He was an entirely unassuming young Londoner of no extraordinary stature, guiltless of any sort of swank, and so naïvely convinced that he was an ordinary mortal and everybody else as gifted as himself that he did not suffer fools gladly, and was occasionally ungracious to the poor things.

The unassuming young cockney was in fact a prodigy.   He could read a book as fast as he could turn the leaves, and remember everything worth remembering in it.   Whatever country he was in, he spoke the language with perfect facility, though always in the English manner.   He had gone through his teens gathering scholarships and exhibitions as a child gathers daisies, and had landed at last in the upper division of the civil service as resident clerk in the Colonial Office.   He had acquired both scholarship and administrative experience, and knew not only why reforms were desirable but how they were put into practice under our queer political system.   Hyndman and his Democratic Federation were no use to him, Morris and his Socialist League only an infant school.   There was no organization fit for him except the Liberal Party, already moribund, but still holding a front bench position under the leadership of Gladstone. All Webb could do was something that he was forbidden to do as a civil servant: that is, issue pamphlets warning the Liberal Party that they were falling behind the times and even behind the Conservatives.   Nevertheless he issued the pamphlets calmly.   Nobody dared to remonstrate.

G. B. S. Meets the Man he Sought

This was the situation when I picked him up at a debating society which I had joined to qualify myself as a public speaker. It was the year 1879, when I was 23 and he a year or two younger. I at once recognized and appreciated in him all the qualifications in which I was myself pitiably deficient. He was clearly the man for me to work with. I forced my acquaintance on him; and it soon ripened into an enduring friendship. This was by far the wisest step I ever took. The combination worked perfectly.

We were both in the same predicament in having no organization with which we could work. Our job was to get Socialism into some sort of working shape; and we knew that this brainwork must be done by groups of Socialists whose minds operated at the same speed on a foundation of the same culture and habits. We were not snobs; but neither were we mere reactionists against snobbery to such an extent as to believe that we could work in double harness with the working men of the Federation and the League, who deeply and wisely mistrusted us as "bourgeois," and who would inevitably waste our time in trying to clear up hopeless misunderstandings. Morris was soon completely beaten by his proletarian comrades: he had to drop the League, which immediately perished. The agony of the Social-Democratic Federation was longer drawn out; but it contributed nothing to the theory or practice of Socialism, and hardly even pretended to survive the death of Hyndman.

The Fabian Society's Rise to Power

One day I came upon a tract entitled Why Are The Many Poor? issued by a body of whom I had never heard, entitled The Fabian Society. The name struck me as an inspiration. I looked the Society up, and found a little group of educated middle class persons who, having come together to study philosophy, had finally resolved to take to active politics as Socialists. It was just what we needed. When I had sized it up, Webb joined, and with him Sydney Olivier, his fellow resident clerk at the Colonial Office. Webb swept everything before him; and the history of the Fabian Society began as the public knows it today. Barricades manned by Anarchists, and Utopian colonies, vanished from the Socialist program; and Socialism became constitutional, respectable, and practical. This was the work of Webb far more than of any other single person.

Marriage to Beatrice Potter

He was still a single person in another sense when the Fabian job was done. He was young enough to be unmarried when a young lady as rarely qualified as himself decided that he was old enough to be married. She had arrived at Socialism not by way of Karl Marx or John Stuart Mill, but by her own reasoning and observation. She was not a British Museum theorizer and bookworm; she was a born firsthand investigator. She had left the West End, where she was a society lady of the political plutocracy, for the East End, where she disguised herself to work in sweaters' dens and investigate the condition of the submerged tenth just discovered by Charles Booth and the Salvation Army. The sweaters found her an indifferent needlewoman, but chose her as an ideal bride for Ikey Mo: a generic name for their rising sons. They were so pressing that she had to bring her investigation to a hasty end, and seek the comparatively aristocratic society of the trade union secretaries, with whom she hobnobbed as comfortably as if she had been born in their houses. She had written descriptions of the dens for Booth's first famous Enquiry, and a history of Cooperation which helped powerfully to shift its vogue from producers' cooperation to consumers' cooperation. Before her lay the whole world of proletarian organization to investigate.

It was too big a job for one worker. She resolved to take a partner. She took a glance at the Fabian Society, now two thousand strong, and at once dismissed nineteen hundred and ninety-six of them as negligible sheep ; but it was evident that they were not sheep without a shepherd. There were in fact some half-dozen shepherds. She investigated them personally one after the other, and with unerring judgment selected Sidney Webb, and gathered him without the least difficulty, as he had left himself defenseless by falling in love with her head over ears.

Their Literary Partnership

And so the famous partnership began.   He took to her investigation business like a duck to water. They started with a history of trade unionism so complete and intimate in its information that it reduced all previous books on the subject to waste paper, and made organized labor in England class-conscious for the first time.   It travelled beyond England and was translated by Lenin.   Then came the volume on Industrial Democracy which took trade unionism out of its groove and made it politically conscious of its destiny.   There followed a monumental history of Local Government which ran into many volumes, and involved such a program of investigations on the spot all over the country, and reading through local archives, as had never before been attempted.   Under such handling not only Socialism but political sociology in general became scientific, leaving Marx and Lassalle almost as far behind in that respect as they had left Robert Owen.   The labor of it was prodigious; but it was necessary.   And it left the Webbs no time for argybargy as between Marx's Hegelian metaphysics and Max Eastman's Cartesian materialism.   The question whether Socialism is a soulless Conditioned Reflex *à la* Pavlov or the latest phase of The Light of the World announced by St. John, did not delay them: they kept to the facts and the methods suggested by the facts.

Finally came the work in which those who believe in Divine Providence may like to see its finger. The depth and genuineness of our Socialism found its crucial test in the Russian revolution which changed crude Tsarism into Red Communism. After the treaty of Brest Litovsk, Hyndman, our arch-Marxist, denounced it more fiercely than Winston Churchill. The history of Communist Russia for the past twenty years in the British and American Press is a record in recklessly prejudiced mendacity. The Webbs waited until the wreckage and ruin of the change was ended, its mistakes remedied, and the Communist State fairly launched. Then they went and investigated it. In their last two volumes they give us the first really scientific analysis of the Soviet State, and of its developments of our political and social experiments and institutions, including trade unionism and cooperation, which we thought they had abolished. No Russian could have done this all-important job for us. The Webbs knew England, and knew what they were talking about. No one else did.

They unhesitatingly gave the Soviet system their support, and announced it definitely as a New Civilization.

It has been a wonderful life's work. Its mere

incidental by-blows included Webb's chairman-
ship of the London County Council's Technical
Education Committee which abolished the old
Schoolboard, the creation of the London School of
Economics, the Minority Report which dealt a
death blow to the iniquitous Poor Law, and such
comparative trifles as the conversion of bigoted
Conversative constituencies into safe Labor seats,
and a few years spent by Webb in the two Houses
of Parliament.   They were the only years he ever
wasted.   He was actually compelled by the Labor
Government to accept a peerage; but nothing
could induce Beatrice to change the name she had
made renowned throughout Europe for the title
of Lady Passfield, who might be any nobody.

For the private life of the Webbs, I know all
about it, and can assure you that it is utterly void of
those scandalous adventures which make private
lives readable.   Mr. Webb and Miss Potter are
now Darby and Joan: that is all.

THE NEW CIVILIZATION

Since the signing of the German-Soviet Pact in 1939 I have been frequently asked by bewildered friends: Is there any distinction between the status and activities of Stalin on the one hand and Hitler and Mussolini on the other: are these three men all alike dictators? And secondly, have these three sovereign states similar constitutions by law established: or is the Soviet Union, unlike Germany and Italy, a political democracy similar in essence, if not in detail, to the political democracies of the U.S.A. and Great Britain? And assuming that the Soviet Union is a political democracy, has democratic control of the instruments of production, distribution and exchange been added so that the government should be, not merely a government of the people by the people, but also a government for the good of the people? Finally, is it right to suggest that Soviet Communism is a new civilization which will, in spite of the crudities and cruelties inherent in violent revolution and fear of foreign aggression, result in maximizing the wealth of the nation and distributing it among all the inhabitants on the principle of from each man according to his faculty and to each man according to his need?

15

Is Stalin a Dictator?

To answer the first question — Is Stalin a dictator? — we must agree on what meaning is to be attached to the term *dictator*: otherwise argument is waste of time. Assuming that we accept the primary meaning of the term *dictator,* as it is defined in the *New English Dictionary* — "a ruler or governor whose word is law; an absolute ruler of the state — and who authoritatively prescribes a course of action or dictates what is to be done" (the example given being the Dictators of ancient Rome) — Stalin is not a dictator.   So far as Stalin is related to the constitution of the USSR, as amended in 1936, he is the duly elected representative of one of the Moscow constituencies to the Supreme Soviet of the USSR.   By this assembly he has been selected as one of the thirty members of the Presidium of the Supreme Soviet of the USSR, accountable to the representative assembly for all its activities.   It is this Presidium which selects the Council of Commissars (Sovnarkom) and, during the intervals between the meetings of the Supreme Soviet, controls the policy of the Sovnarkom, of which Molotov has been for many years the Prime Minister, and, since 1939, also the Foreign Secretary.   In May 1941, Stalin, hitherto content to be a member of the Presidium, alarmed at the menace of a victorious German army invading the Ukraine, took over, with the consent of the Presidium, the office of Prime Minister and Minister of Defense, leaving Molotov as Foreign Secretary; in exactly the same way, and for a similar reason — the world war — that Winston Churchill, with the consent of the House of Commons, became Prime Minister and Minister of Defence with Chamberlain, the outgoing Prime Minister, as a prominent member of the British Cabinet. As Prime Minister I doubt whether Stalin would have offered, as Churchill did, to amalgamate the USSR on terms of equality with another Great Power without consulting the Presidium of which he was a member. Neither the Prime Minister of the British Cabinet nor the presiding member of the Sovnarkom has anything like the autocratic power of the President of the U.S.A., who not only selects his Cabinet, subject merely to approval by a simple majority of the Senate, but is also Commander-in-Chief of the American armed forces and, under the Lease-Lend Act, is empowered to safeguard, in one way or another, the arrival of munitions and food at the British ports. By declaring, in May 1941, a state of unlimited national emergency, President Roosevelt legally assumes a virtual dictatorship of the United States. He has power to take over transport, to commandeer the radio for the purposes of propaganda, to control imports and all exchange transactions, to requisition ships and to suspend laws governing working hours, and, most important of all, to decide on industrial priorities and, if necessary, to take over industrial plants.

In what manner, then, does Stalin exceed in authority over his country's destiny the British Prime Minister or the American President? The office by which Stalin earns his livelihood and owes his predominant influence is that of general secretary of the Communist Party, a unique organization the characteristics of which, whether good or evil, I shall describe later on in this pamphlet. Here I will note that the Communist Party, unlike the Roman Catholic and Anglican Church, is not an oligarchy; it is democratic in its internal structure, having a representative congress electing a central committee which in its turn selects the Politbureau and other executive organs of the Communist Party. Nor has Stalin ever claimed the position of a dictator or fuehrer. Far otherwise; he has persistently asserted in his writings and speeches that as a member of the Presidium of the Supreme Soviet of the USSR he is merely a colleague of thirty other members, and that so far as the Communist Party is concerned he acts as general secretary under the orders of the executive. He has, in fact, frequently pointed out that he does no more than carry out the decisions of the Central Committee of the Communist Party. Thus, in describing his momentous article known as "Dizzy with Success," he expressly states that this was written on "the well-known decisions of the Central Committee regarding the fight 'against Distortions of the Party Line' in the collective farm movement. . . In this connection," he continues, "I recently received a number of letters from comrades, collective farmers, calling upon me to reply to the questions contained in them. It was my duty to reply to the letters in private correspondence; but that proved to be impossible, since more than half the letters received did not have the addresses of the writers (they forgot to send their addresses). Nevertheless the questions raised in these letters are of tremendous political interest to our comrades. . . In view of this I found myself faced with the necessity of replying to the comrades in an open letter, *i.e.* in the press. . . I did this all the more willingly since I had a direct decision of the Central Committee to this purpose."

Is the USSR a Political Democracy?

In answer to the second question — Is the USSR a political democracy? — it is clear that, tested by the Constitution of the Soviet Union as revised and enacted in 1936,* the USSR is the most inclusive and equalized democracy in the world. The Supreme Soviet of the USSR consists of two chambers — the Soviet of the Union and the Soviet of Nationalities. The Soviet of the Union is directly elected by the citizens in electoral districts of one

* See New Constitution of 1936, pp. 86–122.

deputy for three hundred thousand inhabitants, the number of deputies today being over twelve hundred.   The Soviet of Nationalities, with over six hundred deputies, also directly elected, aims at giving additional representation to ethnical groups whether manifested in colour or figure, language or literature, religion or manners, inhabiting large areas of the USSR.   These separate Constituent Republics (now sixteen, formerly eleven) are supplemented by smaller local areas also distinguished by racial characteristics, termed Autonomous Republics or Autonomous Regions, to all of whom are allotted a smaller number of deputies to the Soviet of Nationalities.   The two chambers which make up the Supreme Soviet of the USSR have equal rights, and their sessions begin and terminate simultaneously.   Joint sessions of both chambers are needed to ratify legislation and meet twice a year, and are convened by the Presidium of the Supreme Soviet at its direction, or on demand of one of the constituent republics.   All these assemblies, whether the Soviet of the Union or the Soviet of Nationalities, together with a network of subordinate provincial, municipal and village soviets, are directly elected by secret ballot, by all the inhabitants over eighteen years of age, without distinction of sex, race or religion, or political or social opinion.   For instance the "deprived class" of the earlier constitutions, former landlords and capitalist profit-makers, relations of the late Tsar, or members of a religious order, are now included on the register of voters. I may add that nearly fifty thousand practising priests of the Greek Orthodox Church, together with several hundreds of Roman Catholics, Evangelicals, Mohammedans and Buddhist officiants, were enfranchised by the constitution of 1936.

The Insistence on Racial Equality

How does this constitution of the Soviet Union compare with that of Great Britain which assumes to be a political democracy? Passing over the doubtful characteristics in the constitution of Great Britain itself with its forty-seven million inhabitants — for instance, the hereditary House of Lords and the prerogative of the King to refuse sanction to statutes passed by the House of Commons and rejected by the House of Lords — let us admit that the Home Country (after the enfranchisement of women in 1919) is a political democracy. What about the constitution of the British Commonwealth of Nations with its five hundred million inhabitants? Within this vast area only seventy millions are governed by a political democracy. Even among the self-governing Dominions which are assumed to be political democracies, one — the South African Union — refuses any participation in its government by the coloured races who are the majority of the inhabitants; whilst Canada and Australia ignored the native tribes (when they did not exterminate them) as possible citizens of the newly formed state. New Zealand is the one honourable exception; the British emigrants, once they had conquered the island, accepted the Maoris as fully-fledged citizens, not only as electors, but as members of the legislature and in many cases members of the Cabinet.   Leaving out of consideration the fifty or so small protectorates or mandated territories, we note that India with its four hundred million inhabitants is mainly governed by a British civil service, and though we may believe in the good intentions of our Government to make it into a self-governing Dominion, we imprisoned without trial some seven thousand natives who spend their lives in propaganda for Indian independence, and condemned their remarkable and highly gifted leader, Nehru, to five years' rigorous imprisonment.

The British Commonwealth of Nations is not alone among the capitalist democracies in the refusal to accept racial equality within its own territory, as a necessary characteristic of political democracy.   In the U.S.A. the negroes, though assumed by the federal constitution to be entitled to vote and to represent voters, are by the electoral law and administrative practice of particular states excluded from being fully-fledged citizens with the right to vote and to become representatives. The Dutch and Belgian empires have a like discrimination against the native inhabitants.   Hence, if equal rights to all races within a sovereign state is a necessary characteristic of political democracy, the USSR stands out as a champion of this form of liberty.

Thus, one of the outstanding features of Soviet political democracy is racial equality; the resolute refusal to regard racial characteristics as a disqualification for the right to vote, to be deputies to the legislative assembly, to serve on the executive or to be appointed salaried officials.   One of the reasons for the Anti-Comintern Axis, uniting Nazi Germany, Fascist Italy and Shintoist Japan in hostility to the Soviet Union, was this insistence by the Bolshevist government on racial equality throughout the USSR.   These three Great Powers were all alike intent on extending, by force of arms, the dominance of their own race over new territories inhabited by so-called inferior races, who have no right to self-determination and were to accept the social order imposed by the conqueror, or to risk extermination.

The One-Party System

There is, however, one characteristic of the political democracy of the USSR as formulated in the Constitution of 1936 which needs explanation of how and why it exists, if only because it has led to a denial by some fervent political democrats that the Soviet Union is a political democracy. This seemingly objectionable feature is the One-Party System of government.

I admit that as an original member of the British Labour Party and the wife of a leading member of His Majesty's Opposition and, for two short intervals, of a minority labour government, I had a stop in the mind when I read the following article in the New Constitution of the USSR, 1936:

"In accordance with the interests of the working people and for the purpose of developing the organized self-expression and political activity of the masses of the people, citizens of the USSR are ensured the right to unite in public organizations — trade unions, cooperative associations, youth organizations, sport and defence organizations, cultural, technical and scientific societies; and the most active and politically-conscious citizens from the ranks of the working class and other strata of the working people unite in the All-Union Communist Party (of Bolsheviks), which is the vanguard of the working people in their struggle to strengthen and develop the socialist system and which represents the leading nucleus of all organizations of the working people, both social and state." This means, in fact, though it is not explicitly stated, that no other purely political organization is permitted to function in the USSR.

A study of the facts suggests that when a revolutionary government is confronted with the task of educating a mass of illiterate and oppressed peoples, of diverse races and religions, among them primitive tribes, not only to higher levels of health and culture but also in the art of self-government, there is no alternative to the One-Party System with its refusal to permit organized political opposition to the new political and economic order. The recent history of the democratic Republic of Turkey established by that great statesman Kemal Pasha in 1920 is instructive. Faced with a far less difficult task, Kemal Ataturk copied the One-Party System of Turkey's friendly neighbour, the USSR. But after studying the democratic constitution of Great Britain he decided in 1930 — to quote from a recent history of Modern Turkey — "that Turkey needed an opposition; contrary to the advice of the Party, he authorised an experienced politician named Fethi Bey to form an opposition group in the Assembly, and had arrangements made to see that this group — the Independent Republican Party — secured some seats in the Assembly at the General Election." The experiment, we are told, "was not a success. The various social and religious changes had aroused opposition among the reactionary elements in the country and the existence of Fethi Bey's party provided a justification and focus for the expression of this opposition. There were street fights between supporters of the Opposition and supporters of the Government; numbers of the Independent Republican Party drifted back to the People's Party and the leader himself finally resigned. The régime was not sufficiently consolidated for opposition to it to be encouraged in this way. What Ataturk had in view (apart from the conciliation of democratic opinion abroad) was the education of the people in political issues, for he believed that that education would come from the open clash of opinion in debate in the Assembly. Since the death of Ataturk the project has been revived — this time with the approval of the People's Party. Twelve of the Party deputies were, in the summer of 1939, instructed to form an opposition group of devil's advocates in the Assembly. They remain, however, members of the Parliamentary group of the People's Party, and even attend its meetings, although they may not vote or take part in the discussions there." *

---

* *Modern Turkey*, by John Parker and Charles Smith, 1940, Routledge. "Freedom for Colonial Peoples" in *Programme for Victory*, Routledge.

The insistence that an illiterate and uncivilized people requiring to be educated for the art of self-government before they can exercise the right freely and with good results has been brought out by the studies of Professor Macmillan of the natives of South Africa and the West Indies. An ardent supporter of democratic self-government for the natives of our colonies, he describes his conversion, brought to him after years of experience, of the need for a period of apprenticeship to overcome "natural obstacles to freedom." "It is unnecessary to remind you of the stultifying, soul-destroying effect of utter poverty and prolonged physical deficiency. Considerations of political freedom do not touch the oppression of poverty. That this always existed in Africa is clear. It was a revelation to me to find, in parts of Africa, quite untouched by

This solution of an artificially created opposition seems rather far-fetched. Perhaps the Soviet Union's invention of "non-Party" members, nominated by trade unions, cooperative societies, collective farms and all other conceivable associations for science, the arts and sport, is a franker and more feasible method. By the term *non-Party*, I may explain, it is not implied that the delegate is an unbeliever in the living philosophy of Soviet Communism, as would be the case in the use of the term *non-Christian* within a christian community. All that is meant is that, in respect of the communist faith he is a *layman:* that is (to quote the second meaning in the *New Oxford Dictionary*), "A man who is an outsider, or a non-expert in relation to some particular profession, art or branch of knowledge, especially to law and medicine." These non-Party delegates are said to form the majority in the hundreds of thousands of subordinate soviets, village, city and provincial. Even in the

---

white settlement, or any white influence at all, poverty every whit as abject as that induced by landlessness in South Africa" (*Freedom for Colonial People by Victory*, p. 91, a collection of essays prepared by the Fabian Society, 1941). Hence Macmillan suggested that the superior race who have become the dominant power in a territory inhabited by a primitive race should, before they retire from an authoritative position, educate the native inhabitants not only in the art of self-government, but in the capacity to produce sufficient wealth for a healthy and a cultural life. For a more detailed study of the need for educating the natives in the art of self-government and the maximizing of production, see also Macmillan's *Africa Emergent* (Faber, 1938) and *Democratization of the Empire* (Kegan Paul).

All-Union Congress of Soviets of 1936 which enacted the New Constitution, they constituted 28 per cent of the delegates. "Political democracy in a socialist state," so we are told by the most knowledgeable American student of Soviet Communism, who has lived and worked for many years in the Soviet Union, "demands clearly both the expression of special interests of a relatively permanent nature, and the continuous correlation of all those interests into a unified program which shall not be the 'either or' of the two-Party system, but an honest attempt to satisfy as nearly as possible the sum-total of popular demand. Both these needs are met by the Soviet Constitution. The special interests of the Soviet citizen are continuously expressed in the public organizations to which he belongs, his trade union, cooperative association, cultural, technical or scientific society. All these organizations have the right to nominate candidates for office (Article 141) and will certainly avail themselves of the right. The Communist Party meantime exists as a central core of members in all of these organizations, drawing out their special demands, correlating them with the rest of the country, and leading them in a direction of a stronger and more prosperous socialist commonwealth. . . " *   This unique characteristic of the Communist Party as created by Lenin and

* Preface to Anne Louise Strong's translation of the New Soviet Constitution, pp. 87–90.

developed by Stalin and his associates, as an organization for bringing civilization, not merely to millions of poverty-stricken Slav workers and peasants, released from legal serfdom eighty years ago, but also to Mongolian races and primitive tribes inhabiting the southern and eastern territories of the USSR, will be described later on.

The Alternative of the One-Party System: the Referendum, the Initiative and the Recall *

Let us now consider the present-day alternatives to the One-Party System as it exists in the USSR. First we have the most theoretically democratic of all methods of the government of the people by the people, that is, an assembly of the whole body of adult citizens, or if that be impracticable owing to masses of electors scattered throughout an extended territory, the referendum, the initiative and the recall. Towards the end of the nineteenth century and the first decade of the twentieth century, this obvious type of political democracy was the fashion of the day; the exemplar of the long-established Republic of Switzerland † being cited,

* In the New Constitution of 1936 the recall is permitted: — Article 142. Every deputy shall be obliged to report to the electors on his work and on the work of the Soviet of working people's deputies, and may at any time be recalled by decision of a majority of the electors in the manner prescribed by law.

† There are many descriptions of the Swiss Constitution and the working of the referendum, the initiative and the recall. The most authoritative seems to be *The Referendum in Switzerland*, by Simon Deploige, advocate, translated into English by C. P. Trevelyan, edited with notes, introduction and appendices by Lilian Tom, 1898:

described and applauded, especially by Conservative politicians and journalists; but if free thought and free speech are the test of a political democracy it is one of the most backward of the western democracies, judged by its written constitution, and its present law: no citizen of the Swiss Republic may be a member of the Jesuit Order or of the Communist Party.   If he belongs to either of these somewhat discordant partners in the sin of heterodoxy he may not reside in his native land.   So far as Great Britain is concerned, we have already experienced this primitive democratic structure in the Open Vestry, an assembly of all the male parish-

---

"(5) The prohibition of the Jesuits, which was part of the programme of 1872, 'may be extended also by Federal ordinance to other religious orders whose action is considered dangerous to the state or disturbs the peace between sects' (Art. 51).

"(6) The foundation of new convents or religious orders and the re-establishment of those which have been suppressed are forbidden (Art. 52)" (p. 115).

See also *Government in Switzerland,* by J. M. Vincent: "The order of the Jesuits," it is stated, "and societies associated with it, are forbidden to locate anywhere in the country, and their activity in church or school is entirely prohibited.   The establishment of new monasteries, or the reopening of suppressed cloisters, is also forbidden.   The downfall of the Jesuits in Switzerland was caused by their incessant interference in affairs of state, and the intense ultramontane character of their policy.   It was chiefly their agitation that brought about the conflict of religions which resulted in the secession of the *Sonderbund,* and very nearly the downfall of the republic.   It was determined that in future this particular activity should be excluded, since without the agitators the people would soon learn to accommodate themselves to each other's religious views. . . The introduction of the Federal Constitution, the last edition being 1874, introduced proportional representation and destroyed the party system by the referendum, the initiative and the recall" (p. 275).

ioners for the relief of the poor, the maintenance of roads, the policing of the parish and the levying of the necessary rates to pay for these expensive services. The results were so calamitous that it was superseded by the Closed Vestry, that is, government by an oligarchy renewing itself by cooption; which, in the early decade of the nineteenth century, gave place, in thickly populated districts, to the Select Vestries under the Sturges Bourne Act of 1818, a representative committee elected by the rate-payers, thus excluding the very poor. The referendum of particular proposals to local electors was continued, however, for some time, with calamitous results for those who believe in the extension of social services. I recall that in my husband's L.C.C.* constituency the proposal made by the local authority for the establishment of a public library was negatived by a large majority, the library being afterwards established under statutory authority and being much appreciated by the population. More recent and spectacular experiments in the referendum, the initiative and the recall have been tried in some of the States of the U.S.A. So far as I know, the results have not been encouraging.

Free Discussion prior to Legislative Enactment in the Union

And here, I think, the political scientist might consider quite another use of the referendum, in-

* London County Council, a political division of London. Ed.

troduced by Soviet statesmen, which seems to me to combine the political and economic education of the ordinary man with a unique opportunity for the government to ascertain what the people are thinking and feeling on certain issues, before they proceed to submit the proposed projects of social reconstruction to the supreme representative assembly for acceptance or rejection.   This device is to urge all available organizations, whether governmental or voluntary, to hold a series of meetings to discuss freely and openly the particular policy proposed by the government.   This was markedly the case with the all-important New Constitution of 1936, after it had been drafted by the Communist Party and the Presidium of the Soviet Union.

There forthwith ensued the most spectacularly widespread discussion that has ever taken place in connection with any governmental action in history.   Under pressure of public demand copies of the draft constitution were issued in editions of ten and fifteen millions, until the grand total of sixty million copies was reached, a greater number than has ever been published of any document in such a brief period.   In addition to this publication in pamphlet form, the Constitution was printed in full in more than ten thousand newspapers, with a total circulation of thirty-seven millions.   Discussions were held in every farm, factory, school, workers' club.   Classes met in repeated sessions to study it.   In all there were held 527,000 meetings, with an attendance of thirty-six and a half million people, all of whom felt themselves entitled to send in comments and amendments. The number of suggested amendments which reached the Constitutional Commission, sometimes from individuals and sometimes from organized meetings, totalled 134,000. These were sifted and considered, and the more important suggestions discussed in full session. Some were adopted. Such a plebiscite is without precedent. A people that uses its opportunities of debate so thoroughly has the main requirement for working democracy.

This referendum prior to enactment of the New Constitution does not stand alone. In all the factories and plants and in every trade union, consumers' cooperative movement, and the meetings of local soviets, there is an interminable discussion by the people concerned of what should or should not be done, whether in national legislation or local administration. It is by these spontaneous and intimate discussions of what actually happens or should happen in the workshop or mine, on the railways or in the collective farms, in the school or university, and even within the Communist Party, that the ordinary man and woman becomes an active citizen. This self-criticism — to use the Soviet term — is in fact part of the process of educating the people in the art of self-government. It also enables the national executive to ascertain what exactly are the reactions of all the people concerned to the proposed legislation. A notable instance was the reference, for public discussion throughout the country, of the proposed penalization of the practice of abortion, unless it were needed for the survival of the mother; a discussion which revealed the opposition of many women, intent on living the life they liked, and the support of men, anxious to secure the health of their womankind and the increase of the birth-rate deemed necessary for the Soviet Union. There are, of course, some objections to this freedom to criticize; it may result in hampering the initiative of the director of the plant or the commissar of a public authority. Moreover, when these criticisms are published in the press, they provide the hostile foreigner with evidence of the apparent failure of Soviet Communism. Indeed it is amusing to discover that nearly all the books that are now written proving that there is corruption, favoritism and gross inefficiency in the management of industry and agriculture, are taken from reports of these discussions in the Soviet press, in *Pravda*, the organ of the Communist Party; in *Isvestia*, the organ of the Government; in *Trud*, the organ of the trade union movement, and in many other local and specialist newspapers. Imagine the thousands of bankruptcies, occurring every year in capitalist countries, being investigated not only by the workers concerned, but also by the inhabitants of the "distressed areas"; and their proceedings not only reported in the local press, but notified in the government department concerned in maximizing production for community consumption.   In Great Britain what material they would furnish to the critics of profit-making enterprise.*   But to those who value free thought and free speech as the most important factor in a democratic world, these risks should seem worth running, as they do apparently in the Soviet Union.

The Two-Party and Many-Party Systems

And now for the past and present alternative to the One-Party System: the assumed Two-Party System of Great Britain and the U.S.A. or the Many-Party System as displayed in the German Second Reich inaugurated at Weimar in 1919, or in that much-honored Third Republic of France, established 1871.   First, we note that in Great Britain since the Reform Act of 1832, right down to the present day, there has always existed a third party: during the nineteenth century the Irish Party, after 1906 the Labour Party, and since 1924 the Liberal Party.   This has resulted in minority

* There is also what the American big business chiefs call "the English lovely law of libel," *i.e.* the use by big British capitalists of action for slander or libel to ensure the suppression of all criticism "of the malpractices of capitalist enterprise."   This "accepted technique," to quote the Bishop of Birmingham's protest in the House of Lords, June 17, 1941, makes defense in the law courts so costly, sometimes running into "thousands or even tens of thousands of pounds, which are mere nothing to a multi-millionaire capitalist ring" but are so ruinous to private individuals that no one who is not himself a millionaire dares to risk it.

governments on more than one occasion, which are upheld or let down by a party representing a small minority — in the case of the Irish Party, a minority who were hostile to the Government of Great Britain whatever its policy might be. Even in the case of the Liberal Party and the Labour Party this support of an existing Government is given or refused according to whether or not the policy of the minority is implemented by the Front Bench,* quite irrespective of whether this policy happened to be desired by the majority of the inhabitants. The Two-Party System of the U.S.A., represented in the federal government by the Republican and Democratic parties, with their bosses and their "spoils system," and leading in the individual states or municipalities to perpetual changes in the constitution, sometimes concentrating dictatorial powers in a Governor or a Mayor, sometimes evolving one or two representative bodies checked by the referendum, the initiative and the recall, is not considered a satisfactory example of political democracy. One of the ablest and most recent students of the American political system states: "The present parties have had their life drained out of them and are now mere shells; collections of professional politicians trading the irrational loyalties of the mass of the voters. It is difficult to see any way of improving the existing parties. The Republicans have all

* Party leadership. Ed.

the faults bred by long success and the illusion that all is for the best in the best of all possible parties. The fidelity and success with which the G.O.P. served the dominant interest of the American economic system in the past two generations makes the party, today, less able than ever before to meet the altered demands of the new society. *The* party of business, by its tariff policy, its farm policy, its lack of any rational foreign policy, is now an enemy of many forms of big business. The relationship between the party and business may have been symbiotic in the past, but it is now parasitic. The feeblest industries, the least hopeful activities of the American capitalist system, are those which the Republican Party is determined to foster. Nor is the Democratic Party any better. Much against its will, it has been unable to identify itself with the economically dominant forces of modern America and is therefore less committed to an obsolete politico-economic technique; it has given fewer hostages to old fortunes. But what it gains in this direction, it loses by its internal incoherence. The victory of 1932 is probably meaningless in relation to party fortunes. The nation has given the ship of state a new master and a new crew and given them sealed orders. If by a miracle of political boldness and sagacity, a new orientation could be given to national policy and that were accompanied by a revival of business, the Democrats might dig themselves in, but such a new course would require a degree of boldness and coherence which the Democrats no more than their rivals have had any chance of developing. If they remain content to be 'maintained by the business interests as a combined lightning rod and lifeboat' (Paul H. Douglas, *The Coming of a New Party*, p. 164), they will give way to the Republicans as soon as the major party has got its breath back.   If they start on a really new tack, they will split or cease to be the old Democratic party." *

Finally, we have the suppression of the Two-Party System which has taken place today.   His Majesty's Government is no longer checked by His Majesty's Opposition, which has ceased to exist. The Front Opposition Bench is occupied by a few Tory and Liberal dissentients together with Labour men who support the Government.   The official leader of the Front Opposition Bench is the Right Honourable Arthur Greenwood, a whole-hearted supporter of the National Government.   Hence, today, we have in Great Britain a One-Party System which is (so the Prime Minister suggests) to continue for some years after the ending of the war. Meanwhile the three official parties, Conservative, Liberal and Labour, have agreed not to contest any bye-election, so as to leave the political Party represented by the retiring or dead M.P. in undisputed possession of the seat.   I remember a British

* *The American Political System,* by D. W. Brogan, 1933, pp. 383–384.

Prime Minister who was also a distinguished philosopher observing that the Two-Party System, within a political democracy, is all right "so long as there is no fundamental difference of opinion between the two Parties." Is the transformation of Great Britain from a capitalist democracy to a socialist democracy with its planned production for community consumption, and its elimination of the profit-making motive, the fundamental difference of opinion which will make the Two-Party System impracticable? *

* Further, who actually govern the Great Britain of today? Is it the rapid succession of Cabinet Ministers and their under-secretaries who come and go, or the permanent civil servants? The practice of changing the principal officers of a government department with a change of the Party in power, as is usual in the United States of America, is universally condemned by political scientists as leading to favoritism and even to financial corruption, in deciding who these civil servants should be. In Great Britain the salaried officials appointed by the national government or local government authorities are life appointments, in the higher positions recruited mainly by competitive examination. In the case of highly specialized occupations, such as medical men, lawyers and chartered accountants and sanitary inspectors, this examination is conducted by the professional organization and therefore consists, like the Soviet Communist Party, of a self-elected *élite* who alone can practise the profession, whether they are appointed by the state or employed by private individuals. For these reasons the civil service as a whole may be considered as a self-determined *élite* with a specialized knowledge and an obligatory code of personal conduct, and to some extent a social outlook approved of by the existing government, largely influenced by that of the superior civil servants who belong, by origin, and always by social ties, to the landed and capitalist class. It is noteworthy that some of the ablest of the superior civil servants are attracted out of government service by the offer from great capitalist enterprises of salaries four or five times greater than those of the head departments. During the present war the reverse process has taken place, and some of

Even more sensational has been the fate of the Many-Party System, based on proportional representation and a secônd ballot, characteristic of the political democracies of continental Europe, whether old-established or created by the Versailles Treaty. Why have the majority of these political democracies collapsed during the last twenty years, to be superseded by a constitutional dictatorship of one sort or another? First Italy, then in quick succession Portugal, Spain, Poland, Greece, Austria, some if not all of the Baltic and Balkan states, and finally the two great tragedies of the Weimar Republic of Germany established in 1919, and the honored Third Republic of France; whilst the democratic governments of Czechoslovakia, Norway,* Holland and Belgium

---

the most important salaried posts have been transferred to profit-making capitalists, thus strengthening the capitalist system as against the socialist movement as represented by the Labour Party. Today the headship of most of the new functions of government, rendered necessary during the war, such as the rationing of food, the control of shipping, and other types of war production and distribution, have been taken over by business men who have been and are still connected with the particular type of capitalist enterprise concerned.

* "Norway has no two-party system, but proportional representation. The whole country is not one constituency but is divided into eighteen provinces and eleven groups of towns with proportional representation within each separate constituency. Since the last Great War no party has commanded an absolute majority in the national parliament, called the Storthing, and no government has been a majority government. This means that generally the administration has not been very strong. . . There was a feeling that political institutions and procedures had not been readjusted to meet modern conditions; in many quarters there was a craving for 'more business in politics and less politics in business.' Certain

are exiled from their own countries and have their headquarters in Great Britain.   It is a strange fact that the only constitutional political democracies established in Europe after the Great War, to survive to the present day, are, in fact, the USSR and the Republic of Turkey, both of which have recognized in their constitution the One-Party System of government.*

I cite these failures of the traditional Two-Party System of the United Kingdom and the U.S.A. and of the Many-Party System of other European capitalist democracies, *not in order to pave the way for the adoption of the One-Party System of the USSR and the Republic of Turkey,* but to raise the ques-

---

sections in the press were constantly trying to ridicule the Storthing and the whole political system as not efficient enough. And the complex party situation called for a thorough discussion of the very principles of our parliamentary system. . .

"But anybody taking this as an evidence of budding sympathy for a totalitarian system of government would have been entirely mistaken. It was rather evidence of a growing realization of the waste of energy in Party strife, of a groping toward new means of minimizing the costs of friction in public life, of a realization of the fact that national politics does not mean merely fighting — fighting other Parties and platforms and their political ideas and conceptions, but that it means also (and in daily routine more than anything else) cooperation and coordination." See *I Saw it Happen in Norway,* by Carl J. Hambro, pp. 66, 70–71.

* One of the cardinal defects of the Two-Party or Many-Party System, as contrasted with government by a permanent civil service, or the equivalent, a One-Party *élite,* is that the immediate purpose of a general election, contested by rival Parties, is to bring into office a group of men many of whom have no technical qualification, whether as administrators, or for dealing with such specialized services as national finance, or the supervision of courts of law, foreign or military affairs, special services of education, health insurance and unemployment.

tion whether sociologists have yet solved the problem of how to organize the government of the people by the people, and be it added, for the good of the people? Is the problem which we have to solve the ascertainment of the personal or public opinion of the inhabitants — if they have any — as to what should be the exact policy of the government in the complicated issues of home and foreign affairs; or is it the understanding and consequent consent of the inhabitants to policies originating in the advice of specialists, with an agreed scale of values of what is right or what is wrong, and with sufficient scientific knowledge of what has happened and is happening, to be able to forecast what will happen if certain steps are taken to make it happen?

Will Political Parties survive?

It is obvious that when there is civil war within a country, or international war between sovereign states, the One-Party System with its suppression of incipient revolt or Fifth Column treachery, will and must prevail. Once class conflict between "a nation of the rich and a nation of the poor" within a community or war between sovereign states has ceased to trouble humanity, I see no reason for the survival of political Parties, One, Two or Many, seeking to dominate the whole life of the country on all issues, home and foreign. I foresee a rise of infinite varieties in the grouping of men and women for different but not inconsistent purposes. These associations will include as a matter of course the trade unions and consumers' cooperative movements, collective farms and industrial cooperatives, professional associations with definitely ascertained qualifications for the service of the community such as lawyers, medical men, architects and accountants, and civil servants. There may even be associations of individual producers, preferring a lonely but unregulated life, producing and selling stray articles sufficient for meeting their own personal needs. But besides all these organizations concerned with the production of commodities and services needed for the material progress of a community, there will be organizations for scientific research, for music and acting, for sports and games and heaven knows what else, even for participation in religious rites and ceremonies, in order to live a holy life with the hope of personal immortality or of absorption in the spirit of love at work in the universe. All these bodies will seek to be represented on local councils and the national representative assembly, elected by all the adult inhabitants within a particular area; not in order to fight each other for supremacy in all issues of the nation's home and foreign affairs, but so as to secure the opportunity of contributing their peculiar knowledge, skill, artistic gifts or ethical codes of conduct to the life of the nation. So-called "free thought and free expression by word and by writ" mocks human progress, unless the common people are taught to think and inspired to use this knowledge in the interests of their commonwealth. This will be done by lectures and discussions among their fellow citizens up and down the country; by seeking election to representative assemblies or serving on administrative executives. It is this widespread knowledge of and devotion to the public welfare that is the keynote of Soviet Democracy.

The Democratic Control of the Instruments of Production, Distribution and Exchange

At this point I reach the most distinctive and unique characteristic of Soviet Communism: the democratic control of land and capital. This entails a brief summary of the Marx-Engels interpretation of the structure and the working of capitalist profit-making — the dominating feature of what is termed "Western Civilization."

Karl Marx in his long study of the capitalist profit-making system in Great Britain — the land of its birth — admitted that in its earliest stages it had two outstanding achievements. Through the use of power, mechanization and mass production carried out by multitudes of weekly wage-earners, the wealth of the nation had been enormously increased. But it had done more than this. By sweeping away the network of feudal obligations between king and barons, the lord and his tenant, and the craftsman and his guild, and by substituting for these outworn ties the individualist creed of free competition with the minimum of state interference, Western Civilization had secured for the fortunate few who have inherited, or gained, a secure and sufficient livelihood, an absence of restraint in thought, word and act unknown to the mediaeval world. Unfortunately this same capitalist profit-making led to mass destitution, to low wages, long hours, bad housing and insufficient food. In the famous words of Disraeli, it divided Great Britain into "a nation of the rich and a nation of the poor." The all-powerful governing class of landlords and capitalists had, in fact, refused to multitudes of men, women and children that other and all-important ingredient of personal freedom — *the presence of opportunity to live a healthy, happy and cultured life.* Even more disastrous to the welfare of the community is the constantly recurring unemployment of millions of men, gradually producing a hard kernel of workless people, mostly young persons, who become, as years pass by, veritable parasites. One evil Marx did not foresee. There would be not only unemployment on a vast scale, but a sinister decline of the birthrate threatening the survival of our race as a significant factor in human progress. What British socialists failed to realize was the truth of Karl Marx's prophecy, that with the advent of monopoly capitalism, with its restricted production, and when profits failed, periods of bad trade would not di-

minish, but would increase in intensity and dura-
tion.   Thus the landlords and capitalists in the
European sovereign states would, in order to use
profitably their surplus capital, seek new lands to
conquer in Africa and Asia, inhabited by helpless
natives, easy to cheat and enslave.   This would
lead to aggressive imperialism on the part of the
Great European Powers.   The climax would be
world war, which, if not prevented by an international uprising of the proletariat, might destroy
Western Civilization by mutual mass murder and
the wholesale destruction of property and lead to
a return of brutal barbarism — a forecast which
has been dramatically fulfilled.   Hence the slo-
gan: "Workers of the world, unite: you have nothing to lose but your chains, and a new world to
win."

But what should be the new world order when
the workers were in the seat of power?   Karl
Marx had suggested a "dictatorship of the proletariat," to be followed, in some undefined way, by
a "classless society."   When fanatical followers
argued among themselves what exactly these
phrases meant, and appealed to their leader, Karl
Marx is reported to have observed, "I am not a
Marxist" — which implied that the future socialist
order would have to be determined by the scientific study of future events which could not be fore-
seen.   Lenin discovered, when the Bolsheviks
achieved power, that a classless society had to be

slowly built up by the deliberate but gradual evolution of a multiform democracy: the organization of man as a citizen, man as a producer and man as a consumer. Thus the Bolshevik Party, led by Lenin, proceeded to develop a powerful trade union movement, now numbering more than twenty million members, including all the workers, by hand and by brain, employed in state or municipal and consumers' cooperative enterprises; also of the consumers' cooperative movement, today numbering over thirty-seven million members, the largest and most active in the world. There remained over the agricultural population, the largest element in Tsarist Russia; consisting of a few great landlords and a minority of well-to-do Kulaks owning agricultural land and employing labor at miserably low wages, in order to make profit by the production and sale of agricultural products, whilst the vast majority were poor peasants, always on the point of famine whether as agricultural laborers or as the owners of tiny plots of land. Lenin did not undertake to solve this problem. He thought that it was impracticable at that stage of development to sweep away the profit-making motive in agriculture. After his death, Stalin and his associates persuaded the All-Union Congress of the Communist Party to adopt, and the Supreme Soviet of the USSR to apply, the principle of the collectivization of agriculture embodied in associations of self-governing worker-producers. After

1929 thousands of collective farms opened up throughout the Soviet territory, today numbering well over two hundred thousand. These collective farms had what has been termed a mixed economy. Unlike the agricultural cooperative societies of Scandinavia and the U.S.A., the members of the collective farms are not profit-making employers of labor, whether in their own farms or in joint factories for the preparation of food products and the selling to the retailers. They are associations of agricultural workers engaged in a common task of cultivating the land for the supply of food, whether vegetable or animal. Nor is personal property excluded from this mixed economy: it is usual for each worker and his family to be allotted a piece of land which they can cultivate for the supply of their own food, the surplus being sold in the neighboring free market, where they can buy commodities produced in the neighborhood. These collective farms hold the land on a permanent lease from the government without payment of rent so long as they fulfil their collective obligation to the community. In return for the use of the land they are required to sell to the government a defined amount of the product, for which they are paid fixed prices, selling the surplus in the local market; they also depend on the government for the supply of tractors and often for the skilled mechanics provided by the government local tractor stations. Any inequality in the fertility of the land held by a particular collective farm, or its access to nearby markets, is remedied by an income tax on the members as a whole, and on the individuals who are selling commodities in the free markets. Thus the government exercises a monetary control over the collective farms.*

It must be added that for the cultivation of plants and the breeding of animals involving specialized knowledge and scientific research, there are state farms, either belonging to the national or local governments, and administered with the active co-operation of the trade union movement, as is the case in all completely socialized institutions.

Is the USSR a Multiform Democracy?

Now it is important to note that, throughout the development of this multiform democracy, Lenin and Stalin both realized that it was man as a citizen through the political state that had to be the predominant partner, if only because, unlike the or-

---

* This type of organization — associations of self-governing owner-producers — is also that of specialized workers, such as fishermen and the hunters of fur-producing animals, as well as the handicrafts for the production of specialized articles, and in a few cases of factory and mine workers. These industrial cooperatives or self-governing workshops today include over two million workers and show every sign of increasing. Within the capitalist profit-making system they have been a failure in spite of the devoted propaganda of the Christian Socialists in 1840–1860 or the more revolutionary fervor of the Guild Socialists in 1910–1922. The few that have survived are closely connected with and dependent on the consumers' cooperative movement.

ganization of the producers in trade unions or collective farms, or of the consumers in the consumers' cooperative movement, political democracy represents all the inhabitants of a given territory.   It is necessary to emphasize this plain and indisputable fact, because the supremacy of the political democracy over industrial democracy not only angers the anarchists, who want to be free of all control, by whomsoever exercised, but upsets those who believe in "workers' control" or the "dictatorship of the proletariat."   What is still more surprising is that some avowed believers in political democracy suspect the duly elected deputies of becoming, somehow or other, "dictators" of a peculiarly sinister type.   But it is clear that it is only an assembly, representing *all the inhabitants* on its executive, that is entitled, according to democratic principles, to preserve public order by law courts and police, and to defend the country from the aggression of foreign powers, and therefore to maintain an army, navy and air force.   Moreover, there is the supply of electricity and pure water, transport by land and water, reclamation of deserts and waterlogged low-lying land turned into mud by slow winding rivers, enterprises which, in sparsely inhabited territories, may not yield profits to the capitalist and will therefore not be undertaken. Even more outstanding are the social services designed to provide for the health and education of all the inhabitants, for scientific research, music, art, even games and

sport; in a word, the culture for a progressive people.   All these activities require an income which
can only be raised in one of three different ways:
(1) taxation of individuals or groups; (2) the surplus value over cost of production yielded by state
and municipal enterprises for home consumption;
or (3) by foreign trade, exchanging goods which
the nation does not require (*i.e.* gold in the USSR)
or can make more cheaply for commodities which
they do not possess but require for the consumption of their own citizens.   Hence the need for the
establishment of a planning department (Gos-
plan), perhaps the most important of all the min-
istries included in the Council of People's Commissars for the successive Five-Year Plans from 1928
to 1942.

The Constitution of 1936 based on the Rights and Obligations of Man

This elaborate structure, including a declaration
of the rights and obligations of the individual citizen, is described and laid down as the law of the
land in the Articles of the New Constitution of
1936.   This remarkable document ought to be
studied by all sociological students.   Where it
differs from the two historic Declarations of the
Rights of Man — the American and the French
— at the end of the eighteenth century, is that it
insists on the fundamental fact, that without this
obligation on the part of all the inhabitants, all

the time, to provide security and produce plenty, the right to life, liberty and the pursuit of happiness will be an idle dream for the vast majority of the inhabitants of a given country.

Here are a few of its 134 Articles, in its 13 chapters, which I pick out as defining the structure and activities that I have attempted to summarize. *Article 4* lays down that "The economic foundation of the USSR consists of the socialist economic system and the socialist ownership of the tools and means of production, firmly established as a result of the liquidation of the capitalist economic system, the abolition of private ownership of the tools and means of production, and the abolition of the exploitation of man by man."   This does not mean that the state should take over all the means of production, distribution and exchange.   *Article 5* insists that "Socialist property in the USSR has either the form of state property (the wealth of the whole people) or the form of cooperative collective property (property of separate collective farms, property of cooperative associations)." *Article 6*, that "The land, its deposits, waters, forests, mills, factories, mines, railways, water and air transport, banks, means of communication, large state-organized enterprises (state farms, machine-tractor stations, etc.), and also the basic housing facilities in cities and industrial localities, are state property, that is the wealth of the whole people." It is interesting to note that this economic democracy does not interfere with private property for personal use, so long as this property is not made the opportunity for exploiting land or labor by profit-making landlords or capitalists. Thus *Article 9* provides that "Alongside the socialist system of economy, which is the dominant form of economy in the USSR, the law allows small-scale private enterprise of individual peasants and handicraftsmen based on their personal labor, provided there is no exploitation of the labor of others." Finally *Article 10*, "The right of personal property of citizens in their income from work and in their savings, in their dwelling-house and auxiliary husbandry, in household articles and utensils, and in articles for personal use and comfort, as well as the right of inheritance of personal property of citizens, is protected by law."

There are other rights which are protected by the New Constitution. For it ensures to every citizen not only protection against aggression and arbitrary arrest, but also the right to have remunerative work; for the women the right to a specially elaborate provision for motherhood; for both sexes the right to specified hours of rest and paid weeks of holiday; the right of education of every kind and grade and at any age; and, most far-reaching of all, the right to full economic provision, according to need, in all the vicissitudes of life — this formal enactment of such enormously extended "rights of man" is but the explicit consecration in the Constitution of what was throughout the USSR already very largely in operation. Over and above all this elaborate organization *Article 11* insists that "the economic life of the USSR is determined and directed by a state plan of national economy in the interests of increasing the public wealth, of steadily raising the material and cultural standard of the working people, and of strengthening the independence of the USSR and its capacity for defense."

Finally, all these rights are complemented by obligations on the part of the individual citizen. *Article 12* enacts that "Work in the USSR is a duty and a 'matter of honor' for every able-bodied citizen, on the principle 'He who does not work shall not eat.' " Thus, "in the USSR the principle of socialism is realized: 'From each according to his ability, to each according to his work.' " Once this principle has been acted on the human race can progress to the higher level of communism: "From each according to his faculty and to each according to his need."

This fundamental transformation of the social order — the substitution of planned production for community consumption, instead of the capitalist profit-making of so-called "Western Civilization" — seems to me so vital a change for the better, so conducive to the progress of humanity to higher levels of health and happiness, virtue and wisdom, as to constitute a new civilization. This is not to say that in twenty years the Soviet Union has achieved a condition of plenty as statistically opulent as the richest capitalist nations have reached in the course of several centuries. In spite of a material progress during these twenty years which has probably never been equalled in any other country at any period of its history, the one hundred and eighty million Soviet citizens (excluding the territory regained in 1939–1940) have still an insufficient supply of what seem necessaries of civilization — to name only two, of bedrooms and baths! What is really significant in this connection is the economic discovery that this substitution, for profit-making manufacturing, of planned production for community consumption, frees the nation not only from the alternation of booms and slumps, but also, by ensuring a ubiquitous effective demand in the growing population, from the hitherto incessant social malady of involuntary mass unemployment. As to increasing plenty, Soviet Communism has the guarantee not only of a continuous advance of technical science, but also of the psychological discovery by the workers that the planning system eliminates the enemy party in the production, distribution and exchange of commodities and services. The entire net product of the community is, in fact, shared among those who cooperate in its production, in whatever way they themselves decide, without tribute to an hereditary parasitic class.

This produces an emotional passion for production among the millions of workers by hand and by brain such as heretofore has only been manifested in other countries by the individual peasant proprietor or the profit-making entrepreneur. In the USSR it is the trade unions that most strongly insist on the utmost use of the labor-saving machinery, and who have developed the famous Stakhanov movement and socialist emulation between the workers of one factory and those of another factory, so as to produce more at a less cost and thus increase the wealth of the nation.

The Communist Party: its Origin

To what group of men can this remarkable transformation in so short a time be attributed? For it must be recalled that a bare twenty years ago the vast territory of Soviet Russia was a scene of indescribable misery and confusion; a defeated army with millions killed and wounded; workers and peasants everywhere in revolt; famine and epidemics raging through the land. Five Great Powers had invaded, or were invading the country; first victorious Germany, to grasp more land; then Great Britain, France and even the U.S.A. to help the White Army to restore the Emperor to his throne; whilst Japan was in occupation of some of Siberia. No one outside Russia, except a few fanatical communists, believed in the early twenties that Bolshevik Russia could or would survive. Today, despite violent prejudices against the new social order on the part of capitalist governments and their supporters, all the governments of the world, whether dictatorships or political democracies, are compelled to recognize that the USSR is a Great Power, with a stabilized population of two hundred millions; a decline of the death-rate and rise of the birth-rate; no unemployment, and, so many competent investigators think, a steadily rising standard of health, comfort and culture, for the vast population of one-sixth of the earth's surface.

No one denies, whether he admires or abhors the daily life and destiny of the two hundred million inhabitants of the USSR, that it is to the Communist Party, as created by Lenin and developed by Stalin and his associates, that the credit or discredit of the entire organization of the Soviet Union belongs. What is the origin and constitution of the Bolshevik Party? What is its living philosophy and what are its activities? And finally, what are its defects, or "infantile diseases," to use Lenin's term, which may or may not be permanent?

The All-Union Party (*of Bolsheviks*), which today is its official title, first appeared in 1898 at Minsk, as the result of a cleavage in the Social Democratic Party of Russia, two separate parties emerging — the Bolshevik, the Majority Party, and the Menshevik, the Minority Party. I need

not, in this summary, describe in detail the tangled
history of the Communist (Bolshevik) Party of the
USSR.   The Bolshevik Party led by Plekhanov
and afterwards dominated by Lenin, was inspired
by the Marxian vision of a world revolution, whilst
the Menshevik adhered to the liberal policy of the
German Social Democratic Party and the British
Labour Party during the first two decades of the
twentieth century.   Unlike his Russian predeces-
sor, unlike any other party organizer, Lenin had no
use, within the Bolshevik Party, for mere sympathizers, for partly converted disciples who were
ready to vote for his Party.   The Bolshevik Party
was not a Party of electors prepared to give their
vote for candidates selected by the Party; popular
election did not exist in Tzarist Russia.   The Party
that Lenin forged for his revolutionary activities
became, after the seizure of power, the organization by which alone the revolution, so Lenin believed, would be maintained and directed.   Today
it exists, as the student of political science will
realize, chiefly as the means by which the people
of the USSR, in all their multiform participation
in public affairs that we have described, have been
supplied with a political, intellectual and legislative *élite* enjoying the confidence of the people by
its disinterestedness, its superior training and its
practical insight into the needs of the immediate
situation, able to guide the people's uncertain state
during the first period of its new freedom.   Other-

wise there would have been no continuous guidance, no persuasion, ubiquitous and consistent, of the hundred and sixty million inhabitants belonging to different races, mostly illiterate, scattered over one-sixth of the earth's surface.

Its Organization

The elaborate constitution of the Communist Party described in the sixty-paged chapter of *Soviet Communism* is a complicated type of democratic self-government of which I can here give only a mere outline.   From first to last there is no mention of an autocratic leader whose will is law. The Communist cell, the basic organization to be found in every type of association, industrial and agricultural, scientific and cultural, even associations for games and sport, elects deputies to local conferences of the Party, and from these conferences deputies are appointed to the congress of the Party of each constituent republic or autonomous region, and from thence to the supreme authority of the Party — the All-Union Congress of the Communist Party meeting at Moscow.   So far as its internal constitution is concerned, it is a democratic organization, similar to the recognized professions in Great Britain of medical men and surgeons, of barristers and solicitors, and it admits new members after examination to test their capacity to practise the vocation concerned.   Where it differs from these professional organizations is in the rigor and all-inclusiveness of the conditions imposed on the members, and in the variety and importance of its activities.

"Puritan" Ethics

What, for instance, is the code of conduct for the individual member?   Here I may note that there is a stop in the mind of former Bohemian admirers of the Bolshevik revolution of 1917–1922 regarding what seems to them a terrifying resurrection of what they call "puritan ethics."   Within the Communist Party and among the five million Comsomols (the organization of youth) sexual promiscuity, like all forms of self-indulgence, has come to be definitely thought contrary to communist ethics, on the grounds enumerated by Lenin: "it is a frequent cause of disease; it impairs the productivity of labor; it is disturbing to accurate judgment and inimical to intellectual acquisition and scientific discovery, besides frequently involving cruelty to individual sufferers." This insistence on self-restraint, in all cases where the health and happiness not only of the individual person but also of the community are at risk, accounts for the penalization of homosexuality and for the limitation of abortion to cases in which the life of the child-bearing mother is threatened — reforms which are violently denounced by some of the more anarchic of Soviet critics.   Most reactionary of all, from the standpoint of the libertarian, is the outspoken approval of the lifelong attachment of husband and wife as the most appropriate setting under communism for family life.

Thus the test of membership of the Communist Party is fundamentally that of acceptance of an ideology relating to man in his relation to man, and man's relation to the universe, from which is evolved an exceptionally strict code of conduct, not imposed on the ordinary citizen, a code which all members must carry out, the sanction being reprimand, or, if obdurate, expulsion from membership. It has even added, in its new category of "sympathizers," something analogous to the "lay brothers" of the religious orders. In fact, in the nature of its mentality, as in the code of personal conduct, the Communist Party resembles more a religious order than the organization of the learned professions of Western Europe, such as those of lawyers and doctors, engineers and public accountants.

The Education of the People

Can I sum up the purpose — the vocation of the Communist Party of two million five hundred thousand members, reinforced by five million Comsomols, who are at work in the USSR today? They constitute, it is said, the vanguard of the proletariat, or, varying the metaphor, the spearhead of its activity, in the maintenance of the Bolshevik revolution and the building-up of the state. But what does this mean in practice? At all times more than half the party membership continues at its manual labor in the factory or the mine, in the oilfields or at the hydro-electric plants, on the farms or in the railway or postal services, they serve in the armed forces on land, sea and in the air, with the mercantile marine or the river-transport vessels. The specific Party duty is so to lead their working lives as to be perpetually influencing the conduct of all their fellow citizens among whom they work. They must set themselves to be the most zealous, the most assiduous, the most efficient workers of their several establishments. They must neglect no opportunity of raising their own qualifications and increasing their technical skill. They must make themselves the leaders among the wage-earners, employing every means of educating the non-Party mass in communist doctrines and Soviet policy. In the meetings of the trade union and the consumers' cooperative society, as in the manufacturing artel and the collective farm, they must, in concert with their comrades in the concern, constantly take an active part, using their influence to guide the whole membership towards the most complete fulfilment of the function of the organization in the socialist state, along the lines from time to time authoritatively prescribed by the All-Union Congress held at Moscow and addressed by the Party leaders, of whom, as I have before stated, Stalin exercises the greatest influence.

The Living Philosophy of Soviet Communism

But there is another factor in Soviet Communism, setting it in contrast with the civilization of the western world. It is based on an intellectual unity throughout all its activities; it definitely rejects every remnant of the superstition and magic which the twentieth-century man in the capitalist democracies retains in his conception of the universe and of man's place in it. That is to say, Soviet Communism has a new ideology as well as a new economics. Soviet Communism puts no limit to the growth of man's knowledge. It counts, in fact, on a vast and unfathomable advance of science in every field, but it refuses to accept as knowledge, or as the basis of its code of conduct, any of the merely traditional beliefs and postulates about man and the universe for which no rational foundation can be found, or any of the purely subjective imaginings of the metaphysician or the theologian. It excludes, and dogmatically excludes, the supernatural, whether this takes the form of the primitive belief in good and evil spirits, or the more civilized reliance on a one omnipotent God (whether or not opposed by a Devil) involving the immortality of all human beings, each individual being destined for Heaven, Purgatory or

Hell.   This new living philosophy, termed scientific humanism, is working out the ethics of a new civilization arising from its own experience of social life.   And in that pragmatic evolution of a code of conduct based essentially upon the hygiene of the individual and of the social organism of which he forms part, Soviet Communism is assisted by the essential unity in principle of its economics and its ethics.   Under Soviet Communism, with its planned production for community consumption, the pecuniary gain to the profit-making entrepreneur, nicknamed the "Economic Calculus," the free working of which is the be-all and end-all of capitalist civilization, is deemed an undesirable guide to action, whether public or private.

Scientific Humanism

To quote the last words of the last book of the Webb partnership, in the postscript to the second edition: "The dominant motive in everyone's life must be not pecuniary gain to anyone but the welfare of the human race, now and for all time.   For it is clear that everyone starting adult life is in debt to the community in which he has been born and bred, cared for, fed and clothed, educated and entertained.   Anyone who, to the extent of his ability, does less than his share of work, and takes a full share of the wealth produced in the community, is a thief, and should be dealt with as such.

That is to say, he should be compulsorily reformed in body and mind so that he may become a useful and happy citizen. On the other hand, those who do more than their share of the work that is useful to the community, who invent or explore, who excel in the arts or crafts, who are able and devoted leaders in production or administration, are not only provided with every pecuniary or other facility for pursuing their chosen careers, but are also honoured as heroes and publicly proclaimed as patterns and benefactors. The ancient axiom of 'Love your neighbour as yourself' is embodied, not in the economic but in the utilitarian calculus, namely, the valuation of what conduces to the permanent well-being of the human race. Thus in the USSR there is no distinction between the code professed on Sundays and that practised on weekdays. The citizen acts in his factory or farm according to the same scale of moral and ethical values as he does to his family, in his sports, or in his voting at elections. The secular and the religious are one. The only good life at which he aims is a life that is good for all his fellow men, irrespective of age or sex, religion or race."

The Infantile Diseases of Soviet Communism

At last I come to the question: What have been the disreputable features, the infantile diseases, to use the Leninist term, of the new social order during the twenty years of its existence? Or, to put the question more bluntly: What exactly is the indictment of Soviet Communism on the part of those who insist that it is a step backward in human progress and therefore should be opposed by the capitalist democracies?

There is, of course, the complete pacifist who objects to the use of physical force, whether to upset a cruel tyrant at home or to repel a foreign power bent on new lands to conquer — a living philosophy and code of conduct which neither I nor the vast majority of the critics of Soviet Communism regard either as practicable or desirable as the way of promoting the welfare of mankind.   I will therefore pass it by as irrelevant to the purpose of this introduction.*

The Treason Trials

Let us take the first objection.   During the three or four years from the autumn of 1917 to 1922, the Bolshevik Government had established itself in Moscow and had succeeded in repelling the German, British, French, American and Japanese invasion, of that part of the territory of Tsarist Russia which the Bolsheviks thought themselves capable of defending.   For some time after they had made a formal peace with their recent enemies they were confronted not only by local rebellions

* Those readers who are complete pacifists may be interested in an article by me in *I Believe* (a volume of essays by twenty-three eminent men and women published by George Allen and Unwin, pp. 337–338), where I give my reasons for rejecting the assertion "that all wars are wrong."

but by continuous and extensive underground sabotage in the newly established plants and factories, mines and means of communication, workers' flats and hospitals, by the remnant of the upholders of the old Tsarist régime, all of which had to be summarily suppressed. But this obviously necessary use of force was not the only task awaiting the revolutionary government. History proves that in all violent revolutions, those who combine to destroy an old social order seldom agree as to what exactly should be the political and economic pattern of the new social organization to be built up to replace it. Even our own limited revolution of 1689 in Great Britain, whereby a Protestant king by Parliamentary statute was substituted for a Catholic king by Divine Right, was followed, for nearly a hundred years, by generation after generation of conspirators to whom treason and rebellion, spying and deceit, with or without the connivance of a foreign power, were only part of what they deemed to be a rightful effort to overturn an even worse state of home and foreign affairs than they had joined as rebels to destroy. Thus, when we published the second edition of *Soviet Communism* in 1937, the outstanding scandal, so hostile critics of the Soviet Union declared, were the Treason Trials which took place in the thirties, not only of old Bolshevik comrades of Lenin and opponents of Stalin's subsequent policy, but also of the best known com-

manding officers of the Red Army, many of whom
had been Tsarist generals, transferring their alle-
giance to the Bolshevik Government in order to defend their native land from invasion by German,
British, American, French and Japanese armies;
but who, it was alleged and I think proved, had
begun to intrigue with the German Army against
the new social order of the Soviet Union.   The
most important of these conspiracies was the Trotsky movement against the policy of building up
socialism in one country as impracticable and in-
sisting that the Bolshevik Party should abide by
what was held to be the Marx-Lenin policy of promoting proletarian revolutions throughout the
world.   The success of the Soviet Government in
instituting not only a political but an industrial
democracy, and thereby enormously increasing
the health, wealth and culture of the inhabitants,
and the consequent recognition of the USSR as a
Great Power, discredited the Trotsky movement,
which I think was finally liquidated by the murder
of Trotsky in Mexico by one of his own followers.
Today, and for some time, there has been no sign
of conspiracies or faked conspiracies within the
Soviet Union.   The fear of German invasion and
the consequent dominance of the Nazi system of
racial oppression has made clear to all the *bona
fide* citizens of the USSR the overwhelming de-
sirability of keeping out of world war as long as
possible, meanwhile devoting their energies to in-

creasing their means of livelihood and their defensive power; whilst the capitalist democracies and Axis powers were engaged in mutual mass murder and the destruction of property. When the German attack plunged Russia into war it was immediately apparent that the inhabitants of the USSR, whether soldiers or civilians, men, women and young people, were so convinced of the benefits yielded to the Socialist Fatherland that they resisted not only with reckless courage, but with considerable skill and ingenuity the powerful onslaught of the highly mechanized German Army hitherto victorious conquerors of one country after another.

There are, however, features in Soviet Communism which are either wholly absent in Great Britain, the self-governing Dominions and the U.S.A., or are far less virulent and permanent than they seem to be in the Soviet Union of today.

The Idolization of the Leader

The first of these is the idolization of one individual as an infallible leader who must be reverenced and obeyed and not criticized. This idolization was seen in the popular elevation of Lenin, notably after his death, to the status of saint or prophet, virtually canonized in the sleeping figure in the mausoleum in Moscow's Red Square, where he was, to all intents and purposes, worshipped by the adoring multitude of workers and peasants who

daily pass before him.   After Lenin's death it was
agreed that his place could never be filled.   Some
new personality had to be produced for the hundred and sixty million inhabitants of the USSR,
most of whom were illiterate, deplorably super-
stitious and incapable of grasping the new philosophy of the Communist Party.   Among the
leaders of the Communist Party there ensued a
tacit understanding that Stalin should be "boosted"
as the supreme leader of the proletariat, the Party
and the state.   His portrait and his bust were ac-
cordingly distributed by tens of thousands.   But
this idolization of Stalin has largely ceased to exist
in the Soviet Union of today.   In the village, municipal and union soviets, local heroes are held up
for the admiration of and imitation by the people;
heroes of the workshop and of the field, heroes
of research and exploration, ordinary everyday
people whose heroism consists not in an isolated
courageous act under the stress of emotion, but in
outstanding continuous application of courage and
intelligence, initiative and self-discipline.   The
portraits of these heroes and heroines are to be seen
everywhere.   Moreover, Stalin's recent step down
from the pedestal of the Holy Father of the Communist Party to the prosaic position of Prime Minister, elected strictly according to the constitutional
procedure of a political democracy, has, so to
speak, secularized his status and made it that of
any other Prime Minister ultimately dependent on

the votes of the people. When Stalin disappears from the scene will he have a successor as an idolized figure? I doubt it. The very conception of an infallible or a mysteriously inspired leader is wholly inconsistent with the Marx-Lenin materialist interpretation of history. Lenin would have mocked at his idolized figure in the mausoleum in the Red Square of Moscow. Stalin has never claimed to be more than the duly appointed official of the Communist Party and the democratically elected member of the Supreme Soviet of the USSR. Hence, I believe this infantile disease will die out with the spread of education among the multitude and the practice of the scientific method in all branches of human activities. With a more enlightened electorate and the emergence of men with specialized talents I foresee that the influence now exercised by Stalin will be inherited by a group of prominent members of the Communist Party, of its All-Union Congress, qualified to stand for the central committee and its subordinate councils. This group who happen to become the recognized leaders of the party will grow larger and more diversified with the development of new scientific technique in all departments of government, alike in Moscow and in its constituent republics.

The Disease of Orthodoxy

Far more repugnant to our western political habits is the absolute prohibition within the USSR of any propaganda advocating the return to capitalist profit-making or even to any independent thinking on the fundamental social issues about possible new ways of organizing men in society, new forms of social activity, and new development of the socially established code of conduct. It is upon this power to think new thoughts, and to formulate even the most unexpected fresh ideas, that the future progress of mankind depends. This disease of orthodoxy in a milder form is not wholly absent in the capitalist political democracies. No one suggests that Switzerland is not a political democracy, and yet, as I have already noted, members of the Society of Jesus are not only refused citizenship but are actually banished from their native land, a penalization which has been extended of late years to the members of the Third International, assuredly a strangely discordant couple to be linked together in the dock of Swiss Courts of Justice accused of the propaganda of living philosophy incompatible with the public safety. Likewise the U.S.A., in some of the constituent States, through the device of Primaries, has excluded the Communist Party, and today even the Socialist Party, from selecting the candidates for election to the legislature of those states; while in one or two states being a member of the Communist Party is punished by penal servitude. In Oklahoma City, we are told in the New York *Nation,* December 28, 1940, "mere membership in the

Communist Party is regarded as a crime punishable by imprisonment for ten years and a fine of 5000 dollars. This vindictive sentence was passed on Robert Wood, state secretary of the Party, in October, and has now been repeated in the case of Alan Shaw, twenty-two-year-old secretary of the Oklahoma City Local. In neither case was any overt act charged. Both men were convicted of violating the state criminal syndicalism law on evidence consisting of selected passages from the works of Marx, Lenin and Stalin. Since the ideas put forward in these books were those of Communist leaders, it was charged, they must also be subscribed to by the accused. . ."

Whenever a country is threatened with foreign invasion or revolutionary upheaval, the suppression of sects advocating disobedience to the law, sabotage or giving information to the enemy is a necessary use of force on the part of a government, however democratically representative of the majority of the inhabitants it may be. Have we not imprisoned two M.P.'s and a distinguished ex-Cabinet Minister, and some thousand other fellow citizens? Have we not interned thousands of well-conducted and even distinguished foreigners because they were suspected of a like antagonism to our existing social order? Have we not blamed the tolerance of Norway, the Netherlands and Belgium towards what is termed Fifth Column activities, *i.e.* propaganda by its own citizens of the Nazi system as an alternative to their own type of government?

It is not surprising, therefore, that there should have been intolerance, on the part of the Soviet Government, towards free thought and expression, by word and by writ, of antagonism to its home and foreign policy. How does this intolerance differ in character from the intolerance manifested in Great Britain? As we have described previously, free criticism, however hostile it may be, is permitted, even encouraged, in the USSR, of the directors of all forms of enterprise, by the workers employed, or by the consumers of the commodities or services concerned. In Great Britain no such detailed and personal criticism by the workers employed, or by the consumers of commodities and services concerned, is tolerated by capitalist profit-makers when they close down works or charge monopoly prices, or even if they go bankrupt through inefficiency or fraudulent practice. Moreover, when anxious to encourage historical research, the Soviet Government is singularly open-minded and has just published a translation of the complete works of Ricardo into Russian, which is exactly as if the British Government were to issue from the Stationery Office a translation into English of the complete works of Marx, Engels and Lenin.

There is, however, a type of suppression of free thought by word and by writ that is absent from capitalist democracies but is indisputably present in the USSR. No criticism of the living philosophy of the Communist Party is permitted in the Soviet Union. It would, for instance, be impossible to issue a stream of pamphlets against Soviet Communism and in favor of the capitalist system, such as the Fabian Tracts for Socialists, or the works of G. D. H. Cole and Harold Laski, criticizing capitalism and suggesting various forms of socialist organization; it would be still more impossible to publish a condemnation of Soviet Communism such as the Webbs' *The Decay of Capitalist Civilisation*. Nor would there be permitted in the USSR newspapers and periodicals as favourable to profit-making capitalism as the *Daily Herald*, the weekly *Tribune* or the monthly *Left Book News* (leave alone the *Labour Monthly*) are to the various types of socialism. I venture to prophesy that this form of intolerance — which we term the disease of orthodoxy — will prove to be merely the growing pains of a new social order which has struggled into existence in a hostile world. I may note, in passing, that owing to the increasing urgency of war, our Home Secretary has banned, for the last fourteen months, one daily paper — the *Daily Worker* — and has threatened another — the *Daily Mirror* — with a like fate. I see no reason to doubt that with the increased prosperity of the Soviet Union, at peace with the world, the Communist Party of the USSR, whose living philosophy depends for its realization on the scientific method, will gradually lift the bar to free discussion in the press about rival conceptions of political and economic systems, if only to increase the prestige of the new civilization among the intelligentsia of other countries, and, be it added, to gratify the passion for discussion, day in and day out, of every conceivable issue, practical and theoretical, which distinguishes the Russian Slav, the majority race of the USSR.

The Commintern or Third International

At first sight the least important, but in many ways the most injurious feature of the internal structure of the Soviet Union, exciting the enmity of the British and other Capitalist Democracies, are the highly organized Communist Parties whose policy is dominated by the Commintern in Moscow, presided over by Dimitrov, the Bulgarian socialist rendered famous by his courageous and successful defense during the celebrated Berlin trial springing out of the burning of the Reichstag in 1933. These Communist Parties within the territories of the Allied Governments, have pursued what has been termed a "contortionist" * policy,

* See the angry pamphlet issued by the Labour Party Publication Department, Transport House, April 1940: *Stalin's Men —* *"About Turn."* A more elaborate and documented denunciation of this sudden twist-round of the Communist Party, June 22, 1941, is Victor Gollancz's able book, *Russia and Ourselves.* It is notable that neither one nor the other mentions the fact that the Communist Party is by its constitution dependent for its policy on the

in order to serve the national interests, not of their own country, but of the USSR. In the first stages of the Allies' war with Germany, during the period of the German Soviet Pact of 1939, they denounced the war as an "imperialist war, wholly in the interest of the ruling capitalist and landlord classes of Great Britain, intent on safeguarding and extending the British Empire with its dominion over the colored races of Africa and Asia." But directly Hitler's German Army marched, without warning, into the USSR, they suddenly turned round and started a campaign for an all-out war against Hitler's barbarous Nazi armed forces. How far Premier Stalin and his colleagues in the Sovnarkom and the Presidium approve of the continued existence of the Third International is unknown. In the two years after Lenin's death, Stalin successfully advocated the policy of building up a multiform democracy which would eliminate the capitalist and the landlord within the vast territory of the USSR; and he denounced Trotsky's alternative of organizing, in other countries, violent revolutions against the capitalist system. Hence the foreign policy of the Soviet Government has been, throughout the leadership of Stalin, in favor of

---

Commintern at Moscow; if that ceased to exist, the little group of able men presided over by the distinguished scientist Professor J. B. S. Haldane and the honest and able labor leader Harry Pollitt, as general secretary, could become members of the local Labour Parties or of the Fabian Society, and take an active part in the organization of a united Labour and Socialist Party.

peace, if possible enforced by the League of Nations, and if that broke down, secured by treaties of non-aggression between the Soviet Union and all other sovereign states, without attempting to interfere with the internal organization of each other's countries.   Persistent rumor suggests that he would like to see the Commintern disappear, but, owing to its foundation by Lenin during the first glorious days of the revolution of 1917, he is not prepared to suppress it. *

There is however another explanation for the continued existence of a British branch of the Commintern or Third International, and the continued

---

* We are told in the most authoritative history of the Communist Party — *Outline History of the Communist Party of the Soviet Union*, 2 vols., by N. Popov — that (pp. 61–62) "The First, Constituent, Congress of the Communist International was held at the beginning of March 1919.   It was attended by delegates from Russia, the Ukraine, Poland, Latvia, Germany, the United States, Norway, Hungary, Switzerland, Finland, Britain and other countries.   The central question at the Congress was that of bourgeois democracy and proletarian dictatorship, the report on this question being made by Lenin.   In his introductory speech at the opening of the Congress, Lenin said: 'It is only necessary to find that practical form which will enable the proletariat to realize its domination.   Such a form is the Soviet system with the proletarian dictatorship. . .'"   In Lenin's book *State and Revolution* we are told the purpose of the Commintern — " 'This victory of the world proletarian revolution calls for the greatest confidence, the closest fraternal union and the greatest possible unity of revolutionary action on the part of the working class in progressive countries. These conditions cannot be achieved unless a determined rupture is made on matters of principle, and a ruthless struggle is waged against the bourgeois distortion of socialism which has gained the upper hand among the leaders of the official Social-Democratic and Socialist parties' " (p. 63).

clash of this organization with the Labour and Socialist Parties within the capitalist democracies in which the blame is on the other side. From the very outset of the Bolshevik revolution in the autumn of 1917, the International Federation of Labour and Socialist Parties (known in former years as the Second International) has actually accepted, as representing the Russian people, three hardened counter-revolutionaries, who opposed Lenin and the revolution of 1917, and since then have continued to intrigue against the Soviet Government. It is also a regrettable fact that the International Federation of Trade Unions, representing the Trade Union movement of the capitalist democracies, has refused to accept, as members, representatives of the All-Union Central Committee of Trade Unions (AUCCTU) with its twenty-three million members. It is an odd fact that it is only the International Cooperative Alliance which has from the first to last accepted representatives of the Central Board of the Centrosoyus with its thirty-seven million members.*

* This "odd fact" is explained by the similarity in constitution and activities of the Consumers' Cooperative Movement in the Soviet Union and in capitalist countries; whereas there is a striking difference (as will be understood by readers of the foregoing pages) between the constitution and activities of the Trade Union Movement within Capitalist Democracies, compared to the multiform democracy of the Soviet Union. This disparity of aim is even more true in the case of the Labour and Socialist Parties in capitalist countries, compared with the activities of the Communist Party in the USSR, with its planned production for community consumption as the accepted economic structure.

Let us hope that Sir Walter Citrine by his wise recognition, on terms of equality and warm friendship, of the All-Union Central Committee of the Trade Unions of the USSR, will remedy this disastrous situation within the trade union world and that henceforth the Red trade unions will be represented by Russian trade unionists in the International Federation of Trade Unions.   If so, we may hope that the International Federation of Labour and Socialist Parties will follow suit and that the Third International and Second International will be thus merged in one organization aiming at a new social order within their own countries as well as permanent peace among all the nations of the world.

Britain and Russia: Social Reconstruction at Home

One more question.   Why have I exhausted the dwindling strength of an Over-Eighty in arguing that Stalin is not a dictator, whose word is law, as Hitler is, and Mussolini tried to be; that the USSR is not only a fully fledged political democracy, but also an industrial democracy, with a powerful trade union and consumers' cooperative movement, with a newly invented type of associations of owner-producers in the collective farms and industrial cooperatives, all alike under the control of the central and local government of a representative democracy, without distinction of sex, class or race? And finally, that through planned production for community consumption, and the elimination of the profit-making motive, the Soviet Union has, in the short space of twenty years, increased the opportunity for life, liberty and the pursuit of happiness for the vast majority of its near two hundred million inhabitants, scattered over one-sixth of the earth's surface?

I started this task with the approval and help of my life partner (also an Over-Eighty) because we thought it desirable that all those who are sincere in their avowed intention of creating a new social order within their own country, designed to eliminate the poverty in the midst of plenty, characteristic of the wealthiest and the most powerful of the capitalist democracies — the United Kingdom and the United States of America — should study the internal organization of the USSR so as to avoid its mistakes and learn from its successful experiments. Owing to Great Britain's unified and stabilized population and unwritten constitution which permits every possible alteration, the establishment of this new social order need not involve a violent upheaval against a despotic and corrupt government, as it did in Tsarist Russia. Thus the British people will be able to avoid the crudities and cruelties inherent in a sudden and violent revolution, rendered more ruthless by the intervention of foreign powers in favor of the old Tzarist régime. On the other hand, in order to carry out this social reconstruction, without undue delay, it will be desirable to study the bolder experiments practicable in the USSR owing to the fact that the revolutionary government swept away the remnants of the old social order and therefore had a clear field for experiments, deliberately devised, to carry out their new living philosophy of scientific humanism.   We may discover that many of the newly formed institutions are not contrary to the living philosophy of the Christian religion which the political leaders of the capitalist democracies assure us is the foundation-stone of our own civilization, but are actually more in accordance with the precept of "love thy neighbour as thyself" than the root impulse of profit-making enterprise, "each man for himself and devil take the hindmost."

Cooperation for a New World Order

But this peaceful establishment of an equitable humane social order has ceased to be the main purpose of this essay.   The vital issues confronting the British people are, first to win the war and then to win a permanent peace.   It is obvious that the heroic resistance, over a battle-front of 1500 miles, put up not only by the Red Army and Air Force, followed by a successful offensive, but also by civilians, men, women and children, is helping us to win the war in a shorter time than was practicable before Great Britain's all-out alliance with the USSR.   What seems crystal clear, even if we beat Germany to her knees and occupy her territory and emancipate the conquered peoples, we shall not secure a permanent peace without the whole-hearted consent of the USSR. In order to obtain this cooperation in setting up a new League of Nations for the prevention of aggression, we must treat the government and people of Soviet Russia as equals, without any reserve arising from the deep-seated antagonism of our ruling class to the internal organization of the socialist fatherland. For it is difficult to deny that during the period between the two world wars the ruling class of Great Britain was hostile to the continuance of Soviet Communism even within the land of its birth. In the remarkable book *Ambassador Dodds' Diary* — published after his death — there is documentary evidence that the governments of Great Britain and the U.S.A. were, through their diplomatic representatives, official and unofficial, trying to turn Hitler's aggressive "intuitions" away from their sea-bound frontiers towards the common enemy of Hitler's Germany and the capitalist democracies of the U.S.A. and the British Commonwealth of Nations — the Soviet Union. This would mean that Germany would have secured the enormous resources of oil, minerals and foodstuffs in the Ukraine and the Caucasus, and might have been able to defeat the superior man-power of the USSR with its one hundred and eighty million inhabitants.

Today the scene has changed. Our great Prime

Minister Churchill has secured national unity by the reorganization of his Cabinet on the basis of close collaboration with the Soviet Union in decisively beating Hitler's Army in the west, recapturing the Baltic Provinces, with a possible joint occupation of Berlin by the Allied armies. When this has been accomplished the four Great Powers — the United States of America, Great Britain, the Soviet Union and the heroic Chinese represented by Kai-shek — can render Japan powerless by bombing her cities and munition factories from the Siberian airfields and invading with armed forces Manchuria, and thus collaborating in throwing Japanese armies out of China.

This new outlook entails abandoning the hostile attitude of some sections of our ruling class towards the internal structure of the new social order established in the USSR. For if we fail to treat her on terms of equality as a democratic and freedom-loving people, how can we win the war against Hitler's barbaric hordes intent on world domination, and reconstruct on a democratic basis the devastated states of Denmark and Norway, of the Netherlands and Belgium, of Poland, Czechoslovakia and Jugoslavia, and above all, of the downcast and humiliated inhabitants of the great historic Republic of France. The recent treacherous assault of Japan on the U.S.A. and the British Commonwealth of Nations, and the preliminary victories of the Japanese air force in Malaya, the

Philippines and the Dutch East Indies, is another instance of the urgent need of an all-out coopera- tion with the USSR, with our other ally China, against the barbarous Axis Powers. Whether we like it or not, it seems that, owing to the closeness of her lengthy frontiers, in the west and in the east, to Germany and Japan, the Soviet Union will be- come the paramount military Power in winning complete victory for the Allies. "The whole civilized world," said the late British Ambassador to Moscow — Sir Stafford Cripps — in his farewell message to the Soviet people, "proclaims your vic- tories, and we, your allies, are proud to count our- selves as such. But the end is not yet. The power of the Nazis is shaken but not broken. . . When victory comes, of which we are so confident, our two nations will have the privilege of leading the peoples of Europe towards a civilization of sanity and cooperation. Together we must march forward to that victory. Together we must work and plan to bring about the happier life which their sufferings and their patience have earned for the masses of humanity. . ."

B. W.

February 1942.

THE NEW CONSTITUTION OF 1936

[COMPLETE TEXT]

We are indebted for this admirable translation of the Russian text to Mrs. Anna Louise Strong, who has given a dozen years to the USSR. It is curious that there is no official version in English of the Soviet Constitution, but English is not one of the eleven official languages in the USSR. Mrs. Strong has examined seven translations, all made by staffs of experts: The *Moscow News* translation (MN), the Cooperative Publishers (CO), the International Publishers (IP), the Lawrence and Wishart (LW), the Inprecor (INP), a translation made by the Soviet Embassy in Washington (SE) and a translation made by an English-speaking embassy in Moscow for official use (LEG). The first five vary considerably among themselves but tend towards a sovietized English not always clear to the average reader; the SE translation has improved on much of their phrasing, but not on all. (Note the ungrammatical use of "Union Republic" for constituent republic.) The LEG makes important improvements from the standpoint of legal English, but tends occasionally towards a too-legal phrasing which violates the clear simplicity of the Russian text. Mrs. Strong has earned our thanks by preserving the feeling of the original in a simple, direct and readable translation. Her book, *The New Soviet Constitution* [New York, 1937, 164 pp.], affords the best account of the coming of the constitution.

CHAPTER I

THE STRUCTURE OF SOCIETY

ARTICLE 1: The Union of Soviet Socialist Republics is a socialist state of workers and peasants.

ARTICLE 2: The political foundation of the USSR consists of soviets of working people's deputies, which grew up and became strong as a result of the overthrow of the power of landlords and capitalists and the winning of the dictatorship of the proletariat.

ARTICLE 3: All power in the USSR belongs to the working people of town and country as represented by soviets of working people's deputies.

ARTICLE 4: The economic foundation of the USSR consists of the socialist economic system and the socialist ownership of the tools and means of production, firmly established as a result of the liquidation of the capitalist economic system, the abolition of private ownership of the tools and means of production, and the abolition of the exploitation of man by man.

ARTICLE 5: Socialist property in the USSR has either the form of state property (the wealth of the whole people) or the form of cooperative-collective property (property of separate collective farms, property of cooperative associations).

ARTICLE 6: The land, its deposits, waters, forests, mills, factories, mines, railways, water and air transport, banks, means of communication, large state-organized farm enterprises (state farms, machine-tractor stations, etc.) and also the basic housing facilities in cities and industrial localities are state property, that is, the wealth of the whole people.

ARTICLE 7: Public enterprises in collective farms and cooperative organizations, with their livestock and equipment, products raised or manufactured by the collective farms and cooperative organizations, as well as their public structures, constitute the public, socialist property of the collective farms and cooperative organizations.

Aside from the basic income from socialized collective farm husbandry, every collective farm household shall have for personal use a plot of land attached to the house and, as personal property, the subsidiary husbandry on the plot, the house, productive livestock, poultry, and small farm tools — according to the statutes of the farming artel.

ARTICLE 8: The land occupied by collective farms is secured to them without time limit, that is, for ever.

ARTICLE 9: Alongside the socialist system of economy, which is the dominant form of economy in the USSR, the law allows small-scale private enterprise of individual peasants and handcraftsmen based on their personal labor, provided there is no exploitation of the labor of others.

ARTICLE 10: The right of personal property of citizens in their income from work and in their savings, in their dwelling-house and auxiliary husbandry, in household articles and utensils and in articles for personal use and comfort, as well as the right of inheritance of personal property of citizens, is protected by law.

ARTICLE 11: The economic life of the USSR is determined and directed by a state plan of national economy in the interests of increasing the public wealth, of steadily raising the material and cultural standard of the working people, and of strengthening the independence of the USSR and its capacity for defense.

ARTICLE 12: Work in the USSR is a duty and a matter of honor for every able-bodied citizen, on the principle: He who does not work shall not eat.

CHAPTER II

THE STRUCTURE OF THE STATE

ARTICLE 13: The Union of Soviet Socialist Republics is a federal state, formed on the basis of the voluntary union of the following Soviet Socialist Republics equal in rights:

The Russian Soviet Federated Socialist Republic;
The Ukrainian Soviet Socialist Republic;
The White Russian Soviet Socialist Republic;
The Azerbaijan Soviet Socialist Republic;

The Georgian Soviet Socialist Republic;
The Armenian Soviet Socialist Republic;
The Turkmen Soviet Socialist Republic;
The Uzbek Soviet Socialist Republic;
The Tajik Soviet Socialist Republic;
The Kazakh Soviet Socialist Republic;
The Kirghiz Soviet Socialist Republic.

ARTICLE 14: Within the jurisdiction of the Union of Soviet Socialist Republics, as represented by its highest organs of power and organs of state administration, shall lie:

(*a*) Representation of the Union in international relations; conclusion and ratification of treaties with other states;

(*b*) Questions of war and peace;

(*c*) Admission of new republics into the USSR;

(*d*) Supervision of the observance of the constitution of the USSR and ensurance of the conformity of the constitutions of the constituent republics with the constitution of the USSR;

(*e*) Confirmation of changes of boundaries between constituent republics;

(*f*) Confirmation of the formation of new territories and provinces as well as new autonomous republics within the constituent republics;

(*g*) Organization of the defense of the USSR and the direction of all the armed forces of the USSR;

(*h*) Foreign trade on the basis of state monopoly;

(*i*) Protection of the security of the state;

(*j*) Establishment of national economic plans of the USSR;

(*k*) Confirmation of the unified state budget of the USSR, as well as of the taxes and revenues which go to form the All-Union, the republic and the local budgets;

(*l*) Administration of banks, industrial and agricultural establishments and enterprises, and also of trading enterprises of All-Union importance;

(*m*) Administration of transport and communications;

(*n*) Direction of the monetary and credit system;

(*o*) Organization of state insurance;

(*p*) Contracting and granting of loans;

(*q*) Establishment of the fundamental principles for the use of land, as well as for the exploitation of its deposits, forests and waters;

(*r*) Establishment of the fundamental principles in the domain of education and public health;

(*s*) Organization of a single system of national economic accounting;

(*t*) Establishment of the principles of labor legislation;

(*u*) Legislation governing the organization of courts and judicial procedure; criminal and civil codes;

(*v*) Laws regarding citizenship of the Union;

laws concerning the rights of foreigners;

(*w*) Passing All-Union acts of amnesty.

ARTICLE 15: The sovereignty of the constituent republics shall be restricted only within the limits set forth in Article 14 of the constitution of the USSR. Outside of these limits, each constituent republic shall exercise state power independently. The USSR shall protect the sovereign rights of the constituent republics.

ARTICLE 16: Each constituent republic shall have its own constitution, which shall take into account the peculiarities of the republic and be drawn up in full conformity with the Constitution of the USSR.

ARTICLE 17: The right freely to secede from the USSR is reserved to each constituent republic.

ARTICLE 18: The territory of the constituent republics may not be altered without their consent.

ARTICLE 19: The laws of the USSR shall have like force in the territories of all constituent republics.

ARTICLE 20: In case of conflict between a law of a constituent republic and a law of the Union, the All-Union law shall prevail.

ARTICLE 21: A single Union citizenship is established for all citizens of the USSR. Every citizen of a constituent republic is a citizen of the USSR.

ARTICLE 22: The Russian Soviet Federated Socialist Republic shall consist of the following territories: Azov-Black Sea, Far-Eastern, West Siberian, Krasnoyarsk and North Caucasus; of the provinces: Voronezh, East Siberia, Gorky, Western, Ivanovo, Kalinin, Kirov, Kuibyshev, Kursk, Leningrad, Moscow, Omsk, Orenburg, Saratov, Sverdlovsk, Northern, Stalingrad, Chelyabinsk and Yaroslavl; of the autonomous soviet socialist republics: Tatar, Bashkir, Daghestan, Buryat-Mongolian, Kabardino-Balkarian, Kalmyk, Karelian, Komi, Crimean, Mari, Mordovian, Volga German, North Ossetian, Udmurtsk, Chechen-Ingush, Chuvash and Yakut; and of the autonomous provinces: Adygei, Jewish, Karachai, Oirat, Khakass and Cherkess.

ARTICLE 23: The Ukrainian Soviet Socialist Republic shall consist of the following provinces: Vinnitsa, Dniepropetrovsk, Donetz, Kiev, Odessa, Kharkov and Chernigov and the Moldavian Autonomous Soviet Socialist Republic.

ARTICLE 24: The Azerbaijan Soviet Socialist Republic shall include the Nakhichevan Autonomous Soviet Socialist Republic and the Nagorno-Karabakh Autonomous Province.

ARTICLE 25: The Georgian Soviet Socialist Republic shall include the Abkhazian ASSR, the Ajar ASSR and the South Ossetian Autonomous Province.

ARTICLE 26: The Uzbek Soviet Socialist Republic shall include the Kara-Kalpak ASSR.

ARTICLE 27: The Tadjik Soviet Socialist Republic shall include the Gorno-Badakhshan Autonomous Province.

ARTICLE 28: The Kazakh Soviet Socialist Republic shall consist of the following provinces: Aktyubinsk, Alma-Ata, East Kazakhstan, West Kazakhstan, Karaganda, Kustanai, North Kazakhstan, South Kazakhstan.

ARTICLE 29: The Armenian SSR, the White Russian SSR, the Turkmen SSR, and the Kirghiz SSR shall contain no autonomous republics or territories or provinces.

CHAPTER III

THE HIGHEST ORGANS OF STATE POWER OF THE UNION OF SOVIET SOCIALIST REPUBLICS

ARTICLE 30: The highest organ of state power of the USSR is the Supreme Soviet of the USSR.

ARTICLE 31: The Supreme Soviet of the USSR shall exercise all the rights vested in the Union of Soviet Socialist Republics in accordance with Article 14 of the Constitution, insofar as they do not, by virtue of the Constitution, fall within the competence of organs of the USSR accountable to the Supreme Soviet of the USSR, *i.e.*, the Presidium of the Supreme Soviet of the USSR, the Council of Peoples' Commissars of the USSR and the Peoples' Commissariats of the USSR.

ARTICLE 32: The legislative power of the USSR

shall be exercised exclusively by the Supreme Soviet of the USSR.

ARTICLE 33: The Supreme Soviet of the USSR shall consist of two chambers: the Soviet of the Union and the Soviet of Nationalities.

ARTICLE 34: The Soviet of the Union shall be elected by the citizens of the USSR by electoral districts on the basis of one deputy for every 300,-000 of the population.

ARTICLE 35: The Soviet of Nationalities shall be elected by the citizens of the USSR by constituent and autonomous republics, autonomous provinces and national regions on the basis of twenty-five deputies from each constituent republic, eleven deputies from each autonomous republic, five deputies from each autonomous province and one deputy from each national region.

ARTICLE 36: The Supreme Soviet of the USSR shall be elected for a term of four years.

ARTICLE 37: The two chambers of the Supreme Soviet of the USSR, the Soviet of the Union and the Soviet of Nationalities, shall have equal rights.

ARTICLE 38: The legislative initiative shall belong in equal degree to the Soviet of the Union and the Soviet of Nationalities.

ARTICLE 39: A law shall be considered adopted if passed by both chambers of the Supreme Soviet of the USSR by a simple majority in each.

ARTICLE 40: Laws passed by the Supreme Soviet of the USSR shall be published in the langu·

ages of the constituent republics over the signatures of the Chairman and Secretary of the Presidium of the Supreme Soviet of the USSR.

ARTICLE 41: The sessions of the Soviet of the Union and the Soviet of Nationalities shall begin and terminate simultaneously.

ARTICLE 42: The Soviet of the Union shall elect a Chairman of the Soviet of the Union and two Vice-Chairmen.

ARTICLE 43: The Soviet of Nationalities shall elect a Chairman of the Soviet of Nationalities and two Vice-Chairmen.

ARTICLE 44: The Chairmen of the Soviet of the Union and of the Soviet of Nationalities shall preside over the meetings of the respective chambers and regulate their internal procedure.

ARTICLE 45: Joint sessions of both chambers of the Supreme Soviet of the USSR shall be presided over alternately by the Chairman of the Soviet of the Union and the Chairman of the Soviet of Nationalities.

ARTICLE 46: Sessions of the Supreme Soviet of the USSR shall be convened by the Presidium of the Supreme Soviet of the USSR twice a year.

Special sessions shall be convened by the Presidium of the Supreme Soviet of the USSR at its discretion or on the demand of one of the constituent republics.

ARTICLE 47: In case of disagreement between the Soviet of the Union and the Soviet of Nationalities the question shall be referred for settlement to a conciliation commission formed on a parity basis. If the conciliation commission does not come to an agreement, or if its decision does not satisfy one of the chambers, the question shall be considered a second time in the chambers. Failing an agreed decision of the two chambers, the Presidium of the Supreme Soviet of the USSR shall dissolve the Supreme Soviet of the USSR and shall fix [up] new elections.

ARTICLE 48: The Supreme Soviet of the USSR shall elect at a joint sitting of both chambers the Presidium of the Supreme Soviet of the USSR, consisting of the Chairman of the Presidium of the Supreme Soviet of the USSR, eleven Vice-Chairmen, the Secretary of the Presidium and twenty-four members of the Presidium.

The Presidium of the Supreme Soviet of the USSR shall be accountable to the Supreme Soviet of the USSR in all its activities.

ARTICLE 49: The Presidium of the Supreme Soviet of the USSR shall:

(a) Convene the sessions of the Supreme Soviet of the USSR;

(b) Interpret existing laws of the USSR and issue decrees;

(c) Dissolve the Supreme Soviet of the USSR in conformity with Article 47 of the Constitution of the USSR and fix [up] new elections;

(d) Hold consultations of the entire people

(referendums) on its own initiative or on the demand of one of the constituent republics;

(e) Rescind decisions and orders of the Council of Peoples' Commissars of the USSR and the Councils of Peoples' Commissars of the constituent republics in case they do not conform to the law;

(f) In the intervals between sessions of the Supreme Soviet of the USSR, remove from office and appoint Peoples' Commissars of the USSR at the instance of the Chairman of the Council of Peoples' Commissars of the USSR, subject to subsequent confirmation by the Supreme Soviet of the USSR;

(g) Award decorations of the USSR and bestow honorary titles of the USSR;

(h) Exercise the right of pardon;

(i) Appoint and replace the high command of the armed forces of the USSR;

(j) In the intervals between sessions of the Supreme Soviet of the USSR, declare a state of war in case of an armed attack upon the USSR, or in case of the need of fulfilling international treaty obligations of mutual defense against aggression;

(k) Declare general or partial mobilization;

(l) Ratify international treaties;

(m) Appoint and recall plenipotentiary representatives of the USSR to foreign states;

(n) Receive the credentials and letters of recall of diplomatic representatives of foreign states accredited to it.

ARTICLE 50: The Soviet of the Union and the

Soviet of Nationalities shall elect credentials committees which shall verify the credentials of the members of the respective chambers.

On representation of the credentials committee the chamber shall decide either to recognize the credentials or to declare invalid the elections of individual deputies.

ARTICLE 51: The Supreme Soviet of the USSR shall appoint, whenever it deems necessary, investigating and auditing commissions on any matter.

All institutions and officials are bound to comply with the demands of these commissions and to submit to them the necessary materials and documents.

ARTICLE 52: A deputy of the Supreme Soviet of the USSR may not be prosecuted or arrested without the consent of the Supreme Soviet of the USSR, and during the period when the Supreme Soviet of the USSR is not in session, without the consent of the Presidium of the Supreme Soviet of the USSR.

ARTICLE 53: On the expiration of the term of office of the Supreme Soviet of the USSR, or on its dissolution before the expiration of its term, the Presidium of the Supreme Soviet of the USSR shall retain its powers until the formation of a new Presidium of the Supreme Soviet of the USSR by the newly elected Supreme Soviet of the USSR.

ARTICLE 54: On the expiration of the term of

office of the Supreme Soviet of the USSR, or on its dissolution before the expiration of its term, the Presidium of the Supreme Soviet of the USSR shall fix new elections to be held within a period of not more than two months from the date of expiration of the term of office or the dissolution of the Supreme Soviet of the USSR.

ARTICLE 55: The newly elected Supreme Soviet of the USSR shall be convened by the Presidium of the former Supreme Soviet of the USSR not later than one month after the elections.

ARTICLE 56: The Supreme Soviet of the USSR at a joint session of both chambers shall set up the executive of the USSR — the Council of Peoples' Commissars of the USSR.

CHAPTER IV

THE HIGHEST ORGANS OF STATE POWER OF THE CONSTITUENT REPUBLICS

ARTICLE 57: The highest organ of state power of a constituent republic shall be the Supreme Soviet of the constituent republic.

ARTICLE 58: The Supreme Soviet of a constituent republic shall be elected by the citizens of the republic for a term of four years.

The rates of representation shall be fixed by the constitutions of the constituent republics.

ARTICLE 59: The Supreme Soviet of a constituent republic shall be the only legislative organ of the republic.

ARTICLE 60: The Supreme Soviet of a constituent republic shall:

(*a*) Adopt the constitution of the republic and amend it in accordance with Article 16 of the Constitution of the USSR;

(*b*) Approve the constitutions of the autonomous republics included in it and define the boundaries of their territories;

(*c*) Approve the economic plan and budget of the republic;

(*d*) Exercise the right of amnesty and pardon of citizens sentenced by the judicial organs of the constituent republic.

ARTICLE 61: The Supreme Soviet of a constituent republic shall elect the Presidium of the Supreme Soviet of the constituent republic consisting of: the Chairman of the Presidium of the Supreme Soviet of the constituent republic, Vice-Chairmen, a Secretary of the Presidium and members of the Presidium of the Supreme Soviet of the constituent republic.

The powers of the Presidium of the Supreme Soviet of a constituent republic shall be defined by the constitution of the constituent republic.

ARTICLE 62: To conduct its sessions, the Supreme Soviet of a constituent republic shall elect its Chairman and Vice-Chairmen.

ARTICLE 63: The Supreme Soviet of a constituent republic shall set up the executive of the constituent republic — the Council of Peoples' Commissars of the constituent republic.

CHAPTER V

ORGANS OF STATE ADMINISTRATION OF THE UNION OF SOVIET SOCIALIST REPUBLICS

ARTICLE 64: The highest executive and administrative organ of state power of the Union of Soviet Socialist Republics shall be the Council of Peoples' Commissars of the USSR.

ARTICLE 65: The Council of Peoples' Commissars of the USSR shall be responsible to the Supreme Soviet of the USSR and accountable to it; and between sessions of the Supreme Soviet, to the Presidium of the Supreme Soviet of the USSR.

ARTICLE 66: The Council of Peoples' Commissars of the USSR shall issue resolutions and orders on the basis of, and in execution of, the existing laws and shall verify their execution.

ARTICLE 67: Resolutions and orders of the Council of Peoples' Commissars of the USSR shall be binding throughout the entire territory of the USSR.

ARTICLE 68: The Council of Peoples' Commissars of the USSR shall:

(a) Coordinate and direct the work of the All-Union and Union-Republic Peoples' Commissariats of the USSR and of the other economic and cultural institutions subordinate to it;

(b) Take measures to carry out the national economic plan and state budget and to strengthen the credit-monetary system;

(c) Take measures to secure public order, to defend the interests of the state, and to safeguard the rights of citizens;

(d) Exercise general supervision in the sphere of relations with foreign states;

(e) Fix the annual contingent of citizens to be called for active military service and direct the general organization of the armed forces of the country;

(f) Set up, when necessary, special committees and central administrations attached to the Council of Peoples' Commissars of the USSR for economic, cultural and defense construction.

ARTICLE 69: The Council of Peoples' Commissars of the USSR shall have the right, in respect to those branches of administration and economy which come within the competence of the USSR, to suspend resolutions and orders of the Councils of Peoples' Commissars of the constituent republics and to annul orders and instructions of Peoples' Commissars of the USSR.

ARTICLE 70: The Council of Peoples' Commissars of the USSR shall be formed by the Supreme Soviet of the USSR and shall consist of:

The Chairman of the Council of Peoples'

Commissars of the USSR;

The Vice-Chairmen of the Council of Peoples' Commissars of the USSR;

The Chairman of the State Planning Commission of the USSR;

The Chairman of the Soviet Control Commission;

The Peoples' Commissars of the USSR;

The Chairman of the Committee on Agricultural Products;

The Chairman of the Committee on [the] Arts;

The Chairman of the Committee on Higher Education.

ARTICLE 71: The Executive of the USSR or a Peoples' Commissar of the USSR to whom any question by a member of the Supreme Soviet of the USSR is addressed shall be obliged to give a verbal or written reply in the respective chamber within a period of not more than three days.

ARTICLE 72: The Peoples' Commissars of the USSR shall direct the branches of state administration which come within the competence of the USSR.

ARTICLE 73: The Peoples' Commissars of the USSR shall issue, within the limits of the competence of the respective Peoples' Commissariats, orders and instructions on the basis of, and in execution of, existing laws as well as of resolutions and orders of the Council of Peoples' Commissars of the USSR, and shall verify their execution.

ARTICLE 74: The Peoples' Commissariats of the USSR shall be either All-Union or Union-Republic.

ARTICLE 75: The All-Union Peoples' Commissariats shall direct the branches of state administration entrusted to them throughout the territory of the USSR either directly or through organs appointed by them.

ARTICLE 76: The Union-Republic Peoples' Commissariats shall direct the branches of state administration entrusted to them, as a rule, through like-named Peoples' Commissariats of the constituent republics, and shall directly administer only a definite limited number of enterprises according to a list confirmed by the Presidium of the Supreme Soviet of the USSR.

ARTICLE 77: The following Peoples' Commissariats shall be All-Union Peoples' Commissariats:

Defense;

Foreign Affairs;

Foreign Trade;

Railways;

Communications;

Water Transport;

Heavy Industry;

Defense Industry.

ARTICLE 78: The following Peoples' Commissariats shall be Union-Republic Peoples' Commissariats:

Food Industry;

Light Industry;

Timber Industry;

Agriculture;

State Grain and Livestock Farms;

Finance;

Internal Trade;

Internal Affairs;

Justice;

Health.

CHAPTER VI

ORGANS OF STATE ADMINISTRATION OF THE CONSTITUENT REPUBLICS

ARTICLE 79: The highest executive and administrative organ of state power of a constituent republic shall be the Council of Peoples' Commissars of the constituent republic.

ARTICLE 80: The Council of Peoples' Commissars of a constituent republic shall be responsible to the Supreme Soviet of the constituent republic and accountable to it, and in the intervals between sessions of the Supreme Soviet of a constituent republic, to the Presidium of the Supreme Soviet of the constituent republic.

ARTICLE 81: The Council of Peoples' Commissars of a constituent republic shall issue resolutions and orders on the basis of, and in execution of, the existing laws of the USSR and of the constituent republic, and of the resolutions and orders of the Council of Peoples' Commissars of the USSR, and shall verify their execution.

ARTICLE 82: The Council of Peoples' Commissars of a constituent republic shall have the right to suspend the resolutions and orders of the Council of Peoples' Commissars of the autonomous republics and to rescind the decisions and orders of the executive committees of the soviets of working people's deputies of territories, provinces and autonomous provinces.

ARTICLE 83: The Council of Peoples' Commissars of a constituent republic shall be formed by the Supreme Soviet of the constituent republic and shall consist of:

The Chairmen of the Council of Peoples' Commissars of the constituent republic;

The Vice-Chairmen;

The Chairman of the State Planning Commission;

The Peoples' Commissars for:

Food Industry;	Internal Affairs;
Light Industry;	Justice;
Timber Industry;	Health;
Agriculture;	Education;
Internal Trade;	
State Grain and Live-	Local Industry;
stock Farms;	Municipal Economy;
Finance;	Social Welfare;

A representative of the Committee on Agricultural Products;

Chief of the Administration for [the] Arts;

Representatives of the All-[Union] Peoples' Commissariats.

ARTICLE 84: The Peoples' Commissars of a constituent republic shall direct those branches of state administration which come within the competence of the constituent republic.

ARTICLE 85: The Peoples' Commissars of a constituent republic shall issue, within the limits of the competence of the respective Peoples' Commissariats, orders and instructions on the basis of, and in execution of, the laws of the USSR and the constituent republic, of resolutions and orders of the Council of Peoples' Commissars of the USSR and of the constituent republic, and of orders and instructions of the Union-Republic Peoples' Commissariats of the USSR.

ARTICLE 86: The Peoples' Commissariats of a constituent republic shall be either Union-Republic or Republic.

ARTICLE 87: Union-Republic Peoples' Commissariats shall direct the branches of state administration entrusted to them and shall be subordinate both to the Council of Peoples' Commissars of the constituent republic and to the corresponding Union-Republic Peoples' Commissariat of the USSR.

ARTICLE 88: Republic Peoples' Commissariats shall direct the branch of state administration entrusted to them and shall be subordinate directly to the Council of Peoples' Commissars of the constituent republic.

CHAPTER VII

THE HIGHEST ORGANS OF STATE POWER OF THE AUTONOMOUS SOVIET SOCIALIST REPUBLICS

ARTICLE 89: The highest organ of state power of an autonomous republic is the Supreme Soviet of the ASSR.

ARTICLE 90: The Supreme Soviet of an autonomous republic shall be elected by the citizens of the republic for a term of four years, according to rates of representation fixed by the constitution of the autonomous republic.

ARTICLE 91: The Supreme Soviet of an autonomous republic shall be the only legislative organ of the ASSR.

ARTICLE 92: Each autonomous republic shall have its own constitution, which shall take into account the peculiarities of the autonomous republic and which shall be drawn up in full conformity with the constitution of the constituent republic.

ARTICLE 93: The Supreme Soviet of an autonomous republic shall elect the Presidium of the Supreme Soviet of the autonomous republic and shall form the Council of Peoples' Commissars of the autonomous republic in accordance with its constitution.

CHAPTER VIII

LOCAL ORGANS OF STATE POWER

ARTICLE 94: Soviets of working people's deputies shall be the organs of state power in territories, provinces, autonomous provinces, regions, districts, cities and rural localities (stanitsa, village, khutor, kishlak, aul).*

ARTICLE 95: The soviets of working people's deputies of territories, provinces, autonomous provinces, regions, districts, cities and rural localities (stanitsa, village, khutor, kishlak, aul) shall be elected by the working people in the respective territories, provinces, autonomous provinces, regions, districts, cities and rural localities for a term of two years.

ARTICLE 96: The rates of representation for the soviets of working people's deputies shall be fixed by the constitution of the constituent republic.

ARTICLE 97: The soviets of working people's deputies shall direct the activity of the organs of administration subordinate to them, ensure the maintenance of public order, the observance of the laws and the protection of the rights of citizens, direct the local economic and cultural construction and draw up the local budget.

* "Krai," territory; "okrug," region; "oblast," province; "rayon," district; "stanitsa," Cossack village; "khutor," hamlets of a few farms [in Ukrainia]; "kishlak," village in Central Asia; "aul," mountain or desert village, especially in the Caucasus.

ARTICLE 98: The soviets of working people's deputies shall make decisions and issue orders within the limits of the powers conferred on them by the laws of the USSR and the constituent republic.

ARTICLE 99: The executive and administrative organs of the soviets of working people's deputies of territories, provinces, autonomous provinces, regions, districts, cities and rural localities shall be the executive committees elected by them, consisting of a Chairman, Vice-Chairman, Secretary and members.

ARTICLE 100: The executive and administrative organs of rural soviets of working people's deputies in small settlements, in accordance with the constitutions of the constituent republics, shall be the Chairman, Vice-Chairman and Secretary elected by them.

ARTICLE 101: The executive organs of the soviets of working people's deputies shall be directly accountable both to the soviet of working people's deputies which elected them and to the executive organ of the higher soviet of working people's deputies.

CHAPTER IX

THE COURT AND THE ATTORNEY-GENERAL'S OFFICE

ARTICLE 102: Justice in the USSR shall be administered by the Supreme Court of the USSR, the

Supreme Courts of the constituent republics, territorial and provincial courts, courts of autonomous republics and autonomous provinces, regional courts, special courts of the USSR created by resolution of the Supreme Soviet of the USSR, and peoples' courts.

ARTICLE 103: Cases in all courts shall be tried with the participation of peoples' associate judges, except in cases specially provided for by law.

ARTICLE 104: The Supreme Court of the USSR shall be the highest judicial organ. It shall be charged with supervision of the judicial activities of all the judicial organs of the USSR and of the constituent republics.

ARTICLE 105: The Supreme Court of the USSR and the special courts of the USSR shall be elected by the Supreme Soviet of the USSR for a term of five years.

ARTICLE 106: The Supreme Courts of the constituent republics shall be elected by the Supreme Soviets of the constituent republics for a term of five years.

ARTICLE 107: The Supreme Courts of the autonomous republics shall be elected by the Supreme Soviets of the autonomous republics for a term of five years.

ARTICLE 108: Territorial and provincial courts, courts of autonomous provinces and regional courts shall be elected by the soviets of working people's deputies of the territories, provinces, regions and autonomous provinces for a term of five years.

ARTICLE 109: The peoples' courts shall be elected for a term of three years by the citizens of the district, by secret vote, on the basis of universal, direct and equal suffrage.

ARTICLE 110: Court proceedings shall be conducted in the language of the constituent or autonomous republic or autonomous province, with the guarantee to persons not knowing the language of full acquaintance with the material of the case through an interpreter, and also of the right to speak in court in their native language.

ARTICLE 111: In all courts of the USSR cases shall be heard in public unless otherwise provided by law, and the accused shall be guaranteed the right to defense.

ARTICLE 112: The judges are independent and shall be subordinate only to the law.

ARTICLE 113: The highest supervision over the strict observance of laws by all the Peoples' Commissariats and institutions subordinate to them, as well as by individual officials and also by citizens of the USSR, is vested in the Attorney-General of the USSR.

ARTICLE 114: The Attorney-General of the USSR shall be appointed by the Supreme Soviet of the USSR for a term of seven years.

ARTICLE 115: State attorneys of republics, territories and provinces, as well as state attorneys of autonomous republics and autonomous provinces, shall be appointed by the Attorney-General of the USSR for a term of five years.

ARTICLE 116: District attorneys of regions, districts and cities shall be appointed for a term of five years by the state attorneys of the constituent republics and confirmed by the Attorney-General of the USSR.

ARTICLE 117: The state and district attorneys' offices shall perform their functions independently of any local organs whatsoever and be subordinate solely to the Attorney-General of the USSR.

CHAPTER X

BASIC RIGHTS AND DUTIES OF CITIZENS

ARTICLE 118: Citizens of the USSR have the right to work, that is, the right to guaranteed employment and payment for their work in accordance with its quantity and quality.

The right to work is ensured by the socialist organization of the national economy, the steady growth of the productive forces of soviet society, the elimination of the possibility of economic crises, and the abolition of unemployment.

ARTICLE 119: Citizens of the USSR have the right to rest.

The right to rest is ensured by the reduction of the working day to seven hours for the overwhelming majority of the workers, the institution of annual vacations with pay for workers and other employees, and the provision of a wide network of sanatoria, rest homes and clubs serving the needs of the working people.

ARTICLE 120: Citizens of the USSR have the right to material security in old age, and also in case of sickness or loss of capacity to work.

This right is ensured by the wide development of social insurance of workers and other employees at state expense, free medical service for the working people, and the provision of a wide network of health resorts at the disposal of the working people.

ARTICLE 121: Citizens of the USSR have the right to education.

This right is ensured by universal compulsory elementary education, by education free of charge including higher education, by a system of state stipends for the overwhelming majority of students in higher schools, by instruction in schools in the native language, and by the organization in factories, state farms, machine-tractor stations and collective farms of free industrial, technical and agricultural education for the working people.

ARTICLE 122: Women in the USSR are accorded equal rights with men in all spheres of economic, state, cultural, social and political life.

The realization of these rights of women is ensured by affording women equally with men the right to work, payment for work, rest, social insurance and education, and by state protection of the interests of mother and child, pregnancy leave with pay, and the provision of a wide network of maternity homes, nurseries and kindergartens.

ARTICLE 123: Equal rights for citizens of the USSR, irrespective of their nationality or race, in all spheres of economic, state, cultural, social and political life, shall be an irrevocable law.

Any direct or indirect limitation of these rights, or, conversely, any establishment of direct or indirect privileges for citizens on account of their race or nationality, as well as any propagation of racial or national exclusiveness or hatred and contempt, shall be punished by law.

ARTICLE 124: In order to ensure to citizens freedom of conscience, the church in the USSR shall be separated from the state, and the school from the church. Freedom of religious worship and freedom of anti-religious propaganda shall be recognized for all citizens.

ARTICLE 125: In accordance with the interests of the working people, and in order to strengthen the socialist system, the citizens of the USSR are guaranteed by law:

(a) Freedom of speech;

(b) Freedom of the press;

(c) Freedom of assembly and meetings;

(d) Freedom of street processions and demonstrations.

These rights of citizens are ensured by placing at the disposal of the working people and their organizations printing shops, supplies of paper, public buildings, the streets, means of communication and other material requisites for the exercise of these rights.

ARTICLE 126: In accordance with the interests of the working people, and for the purpose of developing the organized self-expression and political activity of the masses of the people, citizens of the USSR are ensured the right to unite in public organizations — trade unions, cooperative associations, youth organizations, sport and defense organizations, cultural, technical, and scientific societies; and the most active and politically conscious citizens from the ranks of the working class and other strata of the working people unite in the All-Union Communist Party (of Bolsheviks), which is the vanguard of the working people in their struggle to strengthen and develop the socialist system, and which represents the leading nucleus of all organizations of the working people, both social and state.

ARTICLE 127: Citizens of the USSR are guaranteed inviolability of the person. No one may be subject to arrest except by an order of the court or with the sanction of a state attorney.

ARTICLE 128: The inviolability of the homes of citizens and secrecy of correspondence are protected by law.

ARTICLE 129: The USSR grants the right of asylum to foreign citizens persecuted for defending the interests of the working people or for scientific activity or for their struggle for national liberation.

ARTICLE 130: It is the duty of every citizen of the USSR to observe the constitution of the Union of Soviet Socialist Republics, to carry out the laws, to maintain labor discipline, honestly to perform his public duties and to respect the rules of the socialist community.

ARTICLE 131: It is the duty of every citizen of the USSR to safeguard and strengthen public socialist property as the sacred and inviolable foundation of the Soviet system, as the source of the wealth and might of the fatherland, as the source of the prosperous and cultural life of all the working people.

Persons making attacks upon public socialist property shall be regarded as enemies of the people.

ARTICLE 132: Universal military duty shall be the law.

Military service in the Workers' and Peasants' Red Army represents an honorable duty of the citizens of the USSR.

ARTICLE 133: The defense of the fatherland is the sacred duty of every citizen of the USSR. Treason to the homeland: violation of the oath, desertion to the enemy, impairing the military might of the state, espionage: shall be punished with the full severity of the law as the gravest crime.

CHAPTER XI

THE ELECTORAL SYSTEM

ARTICLE 134: Elections of deputies to all the soviets of working people's deputies; to the Supreme Soviet of the USSR; to the Supreme Soviets of the constituent republics; to the territorial and provincial soviets of working people's deputies; to the Supreme Soviets of the autonomous republics; to the soviets of working people's deputies of autonomous provinces; to the soviets of working people's deputies of the regions, towns and rural districts (stanitsas, villages, khutors, kishlaks, auls), shall be effected by the voters on the basis of universal, equal and direct suffrage, by secret ballot.

ARTICLE 135: The elections of deputies shall be universal: all citizens of the USSR who have reached the age of 18, irrespective of race and nationality, religion, educational qualifications, residence, social origin, property status or past activity, shall have the right to take part in the elections of deputies and to be elected, with the exception of insane persons and persons condemned by court with deprivation of electoral rights.

ARTICLE 136: The elections of deputies shall be equal: every citizen shall have one vote; all citizens shall take part in the elections on an equal basis.

ARTICLE 137: Women shall have the right to elect and to be elected on equal terms with men.

ARTICLE 138: Citizens who are in the ranks of the Red Army shall have the right to elect and to be elected on equal terms with all citizens.

ARTICLE 139: The elections of deputies shall be direct: the elections to all the soviets of working people's deputies, beginning with the rural and city soviets of working people's deputies and up to and including the Supreme Soviet of the USSR, shall be directly effected by citizens through direct elections.

ARTICLE 140: The voting at elections of deputies shall be secret.

ARTICLE 141: Candidates for elections shall be nominated by electoral districts.

The right to nominate candidates shall be ensured to public organizations and societies of working people; Communist Party organizations; trade unions; cooperatives; organizations of youth; cultural societies.

ARTICLE 142: Every deputy shall be obliged to report to the electors on his work and on the work of the soviet of working people's deputies, and may at any time be recalled by decision of a majority of the electors in the manner prescribed by law.

CHAPTER XII

EMBLEM, FLAG, CAPITAL

ARTICLE 143: The state emblem of the Union of Soviet Socialist Republics shall consist of a sickle and hammer on the globe of the earth depicted in rays of the sun and surrounded by ears of grain, with the inscription: "Workers of all lands unite," in the languages of the constituent republics. Above the emblem shall be a five-pointed star.

ARTICLE 144: The state flag of the Union of Soviet Socialist Republics shall be of red cloth with a sickle and hammer depicted in gold in the upper corner near the staff and above them a red five-pointed star bordered in gold. The ratio of the width to the length shall be one to two.

ARTICLE 145: The capital of the Union of Soviet Socialist Republics shall be the city of Moscow.

CHAPTER XIII

PROCEDURE FOR AMENDING THE CONSTITUTION

ARTICLE 146: Amendments to the Constitution of the USSR shall be effected only by decisions of the Supreme Soviet of the USSR, adopted by a majority of not less than two-thirds of the votes in each of its chambers.

PRESIDIUM OF THE EIGHTH EXTRAORDINARY CONGRESS OF SOVIETS OF THE UNION OF SOVIET SOCIALIST REPUBLICS

N. Aitakov

V. Akhun-Babayev

I. Akulov

A. Andreyev

V. Bluecher

S. Budyonny

A. Chervyakov

V. Chubar

R. Eiche

L. Kaganovich

M. Kalinin

N. Krushchev

A. Kiselev

S. Kosior

M. Litvinov

P. Lyubchenko

A. Mikoyan

V. Molotov

G. Musabekov

G. Ordjonikidze

G. Petrovsky

P. Postyshev

A. Rakhimbayev

Y. Rudzutak

N. Shvernik

J. Stalin

D. Sulimov

K. Voroshilov

N. Yeznov

A. Zhdanov

THE KREMLIN, MOSCOW
December 5, 1936

Postscript

THE RIGHTS AND BASIC DUTIES OF MAN AS LAID DOWN BY THE CONSTITUTION OF THE USSR, 1936

WE now add our own summary of the Constitution, not in the Russian phraseology, but in terms enabling the British or American reader more easily to comprehend its purport; and not following the order of the legal text but rearranged so as to bring out its character as a new Declaration of the Rights of Man.

The Twelve Tables of the Law

I. The Right to work, and to be enabled to live by the work that must be found for all able-bodied adults, with their own option, alternatively, to join in independent cooperative productive societies, either in industry, agriculture or fishing, or to work individually on their own account, without the employment of hired labor.

II. The Right to leisure, by statutory limitation of the hours of employment in office, factory, mill or mine; together with the provision of paid holidays and of all approved means of happily using the leisure so ensured.

III. The Right of those who work at wages or salary by hand or by brain, and of their incapacitated dependants, collectively, to the entire net product of the labor so employed throughout the whole USSR, as annually ascertained.

IV. The Right to positive health of body and mind, so far as this can be secured by the widest possible use of preventive and curative medicine and surgery, and of public sanitation, with wages in sickness and incapacity without waiting interval or time limit; and the ensuring of adequate nutrition and physical as well as mental training of all infants, children and adolescents.

V. The Right of Women to fulfil the function of motherhood with all possible alleviation of the physical suffering involved; without pecuniary sacrifice or burden, and further aided by universally organized provision for the care of infants and children.

VI. The Right to education equally for all races, without limit or fee, for persons of any age and either sex, with maintenance in suitable cases.

VII. The Right to prompt and adequate provision for the family on the death of any breadwinner or pensioner; with universally gratuitous funeral, and instant succor of the home.

VIII. The Right to superannuation at a definite age before senility or upon previous breakdown, with adequate non-contributory pension.

IX. The Right to freedom of speech, freedom of assembly and of holding mass meetings, freedom of street processions and demonstrations and freedom of the press [from domination by capitalist, financial or counter-revolutionary ownership or control]. These "rights of the citizens" by Article

125 "are ensured *by placing at the disposal of the toilers and their organizations*" [including trade unions, cooperative societies, sport and other voluntary societies] printing presses, supplies of paper, public buildings, and other material requisites for the exercise of these rights; as well as by the prohibition of private profit-making and exploitation.

X. The Right to criticize every branch of the public administration, and to agitate for its improvement, by groups and associations of divers kinds, such as trade unions, cooperative societies and cultural associations, by speeches at public meetings and by printed matter — yet without any organization of merely political groups having no other common interest than public criticism or opposition, and without permission to individuals or factions to obstruct the *execution* of what has been finally decided on by the supreme elected legislature.

XI. The Right to elect, irrespective of nationality, race, sex or color; freely, directly, secretly, equally and universally; from 18 years of age; to all governing assemblies from the lowest to the highest, without pecuniary, residential or other limiting qualifications; candidates being put forward by non-party groups of every description, as well as by the Vocation of Leadership known as the Communist Party. This will produce an electorate numbering actually 55 per cent of the census population, as compared with one of less than 40 per cent in the United States and Great Britain, reduced as those are by requirements of residence and specific registration.

XII. The Right to inviolability of the person, and of his correspondence. The right to be free from arbitrary arrest, as in other continental administrations, will not have what is so much cherished in England, the special protection of that unique British peculiarity, the Habeas Corpus Act. But (Article 127) "the citizens of the USSR are guaranteed inviolability of person. No person may be placed under arrest except by decision of a court or with the sanction of the judicial department of the State Attorney," which is now made independent of the executive.

THE BASIC DUTIES OF MAN

Unlike all other Declarations of the Rights of Man, notably the historic American Declaration of the Rights of Man in 1776, and the French Revolutionary Declaration of 1793, the Soviet Constitution of 1936 supplements the Rights of Man by the Basic Duties of Man to the community in which he lives and has his being.

First and most outstanding is Article 12: "Work in the USSR is a duty, a matter of honor, for every able-bodied citizen. He who does not work shall not eat." This duty *not to be a parasite,* living on the work of other men, is strikingly absent in Capitalist and Landlord Countries, whether democracies or oligarchies, conservative or liberal. In normal times, the so-called "leisured classes" are envied and honored by their fellow men, they are never penalized.

But this is not all. In Articles 131, 132, 133 and 134, all citizens, male and female, young and old, are instructed to "strengthen public-socialist property, to regard it as the source of the wealth and power of the fatherland, of the health and happiness, the prosperity and culture of a working people. It is unnecessary to add that military service is the duty of all citizens."

"Treason to the Homeland, violation of the oath, desertion to the enemy, espionage, are to be punished with the full severity of the law." Thus there were no Quislings in the USSR, no Fifth Column, as there were in Denmark, Norway and Holland, and, above all, in the much honored Republic of France. These undesirable citizens had been dealt with in the much abused Moscow Trials of the thirties.

Perhaps it is this unique emphasis on the *Duties of Man* as a necessary complement to the Rights of Man which is the peculiar characteristic of the Soviet Constitution of 1936. It explains why the defeated, starving, illiterate inhabitants of Tsarist Russia became in the course of twenty years the relatively comfortable and cultured, healthy and

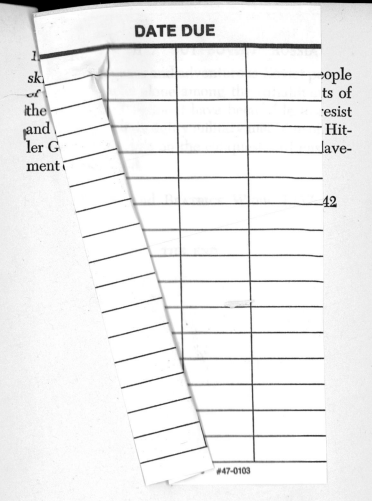

DATE DUE

#47-0103

I... sk... of... the... and... ler G... ment...

...OVIET RUSSIA

...eople ...ts of ...resist ...Hit- ...lave-

42